Vision in Vertebrates

Vision in Vertebrates

KATHARINE TANSLEY D.Sc.

CHAPMAN AND HALL LTD

11 NEW FETTER LANE LONDON EC4

First published 1965
© *Katharine Tansley 1965*
Printed in Great Britain
by Cox & Wyman Ltd.,
London, Fakenham and
Reading.

Acknowledgements

Permission to reproduce the undermentioned figures is gratefully acknowledged by the author:

Figures 3, 5, 12, 14, 16, 25, 26 and 33 are from *The Vertebrate Eye* by G. L. Walls (Hafner Publishing Co.)

Figures 2 and 4 are from *The Anatomy of the Eye and Orbit* 3rd edition by E. Wolf (H. K. Lewis & Co. Ltd.)

Figure 10 is from *Les Yeux et la Vision des Vertébrés* by A. Rochon-Duvigneaud (Masson et Cie, Paris)

Figure 18 is from *Sensory Mechanism of the Retina* by R. Granit (Oxford University Press and Hafner Publishing Co.)

Figure 19 is from *Pflüger's Arch.*, Vol. 259 (E. Dodt and J. Heck)

Figures 20 and 21 are from *The Eye* (ed. Davson) Vol 2. H. J. A. Dartnall (Academic Press)

Figure 39 is from *J. opt. Soc. America*, Vol. 43 (L. C. Thomson and W. D. Wright)

Contents

Plates

1. The Vertebrate Eye

Man, with his highly developed visual consciousness, is sometimes spoken of as having the most highly developed eyes in the animal kingdom. The medieval falconer knew better. He kept a caged shrike on his saddlebow when out hawking, and when the bird reacted with terror he knew his falcon was at hand even when he could not see it himself. Such ideas are not entertained with regard to the other sense organs. Everyone is ready to admit that some animals have better hearing than ours and that many have a much more useful sense of smell than we can claim. Not only can most diurnal birds see farther than we can but cats, and probably most nocturnal animals, can see better in the dark. On the whole, animals have developed the eyes which will be most useful to them under the conditions in which they live although, of course, some are far more dependent upon their eyes than others which rely instead on other senses such as touch and smell.

The basic pattern of all vertebrate eyes is much the same. Figure 1 is a diagram based on the anatomy of the human eye. If one does not press the analogy too far it is useful to think of the vertebrate eye as a camera in which the 'lens' is formed by the cornea and crystalline lens in land animals and by the lens alone in aquatic animals where the cornea is eliminated as a refracting surface by the surrounding water. This 'lens' throws an inverted image on a 'sensitive screen' represented by the retina. Here light energy is transformed, in a way of which we know little or nothing, so that nerve impulses are produced. These are finally conducted up the optic nerve to the brain where they give rise to visual sensations. The whole interior of the eye is darkened by the heavily pigmented choroid coat so that internal reflexions do not blur or multiply the retinal image. The eyelids can be thought of as representing the camera shutter and the pupil as the diaphragm aperture which regulates the amount of light

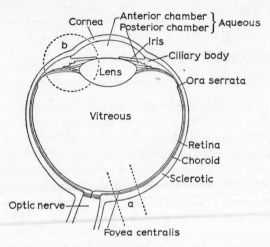

FIG. 1. Diagram of the vertebrate eye. Simplified diagram based on a section through the middle of the human eye.

entering the interior. Finally, the whole apparatus can be focused to produce equally sharp images of external objects at different distances. In the eye this is called accommodation.

The general shape of the vertebrate eye is that of a cricket ball with a watchglass superimposed upon it, although the relative diameters of the two parts vary very much according to the animal's visual requirements. The outer coat is a tough fibrous structure called the sclera and this is continuous in front with the cornea. The cornea (the watchglass) is transparent to allow light to enter the eye. In land animals good vision is largely dependent on the optical perfection of the anterior surface of the cornea and since this surface is exposed it must be well protected. This is done by the lids and by the secretion of tear fluid. The lids are composed of plates of compressed fibrous tissue containing muscles and glands; they close reflexly at the approach of a foreign body, if the cornea is touched or if the light is too intense. Some animals do not have eyelids but a 'spectacle' instead, usually a covering of transparent skin continuous with the skin of the head. Many animals with eyelids have a nictitating membrane, or third eyelid, which is composed of transparent or semi-transparent tissue and can be drawn horizontally across the eye between the other two lids. The composition of the tear fluid varies in different animals. It is secreted by the lachrimal and Harderian glands and irrigates the anterior surface of the cornea and the inner surface of the eyelids. It washes dust and other foreign bodies out of the eye and, in some aquatic mammals such as seals, protects the cornea from salt water.

The sclera is a tough structure serving as a protective coat to the eyes. The contents of the eyeball are at a pressure higher than that of the atmosphere (about 25 mm Hg in man) and the healthy sclera is tough enough to resist this intra-ocular pressure. Certain blood vessels and nerves pierce the sclera in order to serve the metabolic and other needs of the eye. The largest of these is the optic nerve, the fibres of which pass through a lattice-work of scleral tissue known as the *lamina cribrosa*. The development of the *lamina cribrosa* depends on whether the animal concerned has good vision or poor. In animals with good vision it is well developed and successfully withstands the intra-ocular pressure, but in animals such as rabbits or rats whose vision is indifferent it is poorly developed and the intraocular pressure may cause a 'cupping' of the nerve head within the eye. This cupping apparently always occurs in rabbits [180].

The sclera is lined on the inside by the choroid, a heavily pigmented and highly vascular coat which lies between the sclera and the retina. The choroidal vessels supply the nutrition for the retinal visual cells and these degenerate if the choroidal circulation is cut off for any length of time [153]. The choroidal pigmentation prevents back scattering of light within the eye and, therefore, helps towards the formation of a sharp image on the retina. Many nocturnal animals have an additional structure between the choroid and the retina. This is the tapetum which may be developed either from the choroid or the retina. It is a highly organized tissue which reflects light back on to the visual cells. A tapetum must usually have the effect of spoiling the perfection of the retinal image, but it does allow the light to pass twice through the visual cells and so to increase their sensitivity. A tapetum is seldom present in diurnal animals which usually have good vision.

In the region immediately behind the corneo-scleral junction the retina and pigment epithelium are modified and enlarged to form the ciliary body (Plate 1) which consists of a stroma, some glandular tissue and the ciliary muscle. From the ciliary body there arises the iris with, in addition to the ectodermal component from the retina, a mesodermal component from the choroid. The choroid layer faces outward and is visible through the cornea; it is usually pigmented and gives the colour to the eye. If this pigment is lacking, that of the ectodermal layer shows through and the iris appears blue. Completely unpigmented eyes are only seen in albinos and they look pink because the blood vessels are then visible. The iris is a circular structure with a central aperture which is the pupil. The size of this aperture can be varied in many species by contractile elements in the iris tissue. Some of these are fully developed involuntary muscle fibres and are organized into a ring-shaped sphincter closely surrounding the pupil. Contraction of this sphincter reduces the size of the aperture. In man the dilator fibres are not proper muscle fibres but are modified tissue elements developed from the anterior face of the retinal part of the iris. In birds, which have very active pupils, both sphincter and dilatator are formed of striated muscle fibres and may be under voluntary control. In other animals (i.e. teleost fish) the iris muscles are poorly developed and the pupil nearly, if not quite, immobile. In such species, as we shall see later, there are other means of protecting the visual cells from excessive illumination. The function of the iris is to regulate the amount of light reaching the retina and it therefore shows a reflex contraction of the sphincter, thus decreasing the pupil diameter, when the light is bright, and a reflex relaxation with increase in the aperture when the light is dim. Contraction of the iris also increases the sharpness of the retinal image by preventing light from passing through the less optically perfect lens periphery. In most animals the pupil is circular even when contracted but in some nocturnal animals, such as the cat and nocturnal lizards and snakes, which like to bask in the sun, the pupil closes to a vertical slit. A circular aperture can never close as completely as a slit one and a slit pupil is a device for giving extra protection to a sensitive retina. In some species, notably the ungulates, the pupil is horizontally oval and never closes completely. More bizarre pupil shapes are to be found among the amphibia and in some elasmobranch fishes.

The ciliary body lies behind the iris and is normally concealed by it. It is another circular body and is heavily pigmented and very vascular. On its inner surface there are many radially arranged fin-like processes known as the ciliary processes. These form a large surface from which the intra-ocular fluid is secreted. The ciliary body usually contains muscle fibres, contraction of which decreases the diameter of the central aperture. We shall discuss this muscular mechanism in detail when we come to consider the various mechanisms of accommodation.

The crystalline lens lies behind the iris in the aperture of the ciliary body. It is supported to some extent by the iris in front and the vitreous body behind. Its chief support, however, is supplied by the suspensory ligament or zonule of Zinn which is a series of fine transparent fibres cemented together to form a continuous circular sheet. These fibres arise from the surface of the ciliary epithelium and run forward, each one between two adjacent ciliary processes, to fuse with the lens capsule. The lens itself is composed of a central nucleus and external cortex of which the former is older and has a lower metabolism. The body of the lens is enclosed in an elastic capsule which, in mammals at least, varies in thickness round its circumference, being thinner at the anterior and posterior poles (see Figure 14 in Chapter 7). In land-living species the cornea is the main refracting tissue in the eye and the lens acts only as a fine adjustment, altering the focal length of the whole optical system according to whether far or near vision is required. This alteration is called accommodation and is brought about either by altering the shape of the lens (mammals, birds, etc.) or its position (fish). The size and shape of the lens depends on the visual requirements of its owner. It is smaller and flatter in diurnal species while in nocturnal animals it is big and spherical and occupies a large part of the interior of the eyeball. In fish, where the lens is the only refracting structure, it is also spherical (Figure 2). The crystalline lens is subject to some of the

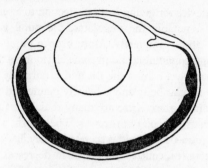

FIG. 2. The eye of a fish. Section through the eye of a teleost fish to show the spherical lens [208].

optical defects of man-made lenses. Amongst these is spherical aberration. The power of a spherical lens is greater at the periphery than at the centre so that the image formed by the periphery is nearer to the lens than that formed by the centre. When very distinct vision of small objects is required the pupil contracts cutting off the light rays from the more highly refractive lens periphery. The eye also suffers from chromatic aberration. This is due to the fact that the shorter the wave-length of light the more refrangible it is, so that the short-wave (blue) part of the spectrum comes to an earlier focus than the long-wave (red) part. The eye minimizes this defect by normally focusing on the middle (yellow) wave-lengths when viewing a source of white light. Diurnal eyes with good vision also contain yellow filters in some form or another (see Chapter 4) which absorb the shortest visible wave-lengths, so reducing the effect of chromatic aberration. One can appreciate the chromatic aberration of the eye by looking at a point source of white light through cobalt glass. This glass transmits only blue and red rays and both cannot be brought into focus at the same time.

Except in well-developed nocturnal eyes where the lens is very big, the greater bulk of the eyeball is occupied by the vitreous body. This lies behind the lens and is composed of a thin transparent jelly usually of about the consistency of raw white of egg. In some species, such as the bush baby (*Galago*), the vitreous is much more fluid, but the reason for this is not known. Birds have a particularly viscous vitreous because the lens needs additional support owing to the special avian method of accommodation. The vitreous body is made up of a very fine network of ultra-microscopic collagen fibres holding intra-ocular fluid in its interstices. Ninety-nine per cent of the vitreous body is water. The vitreous is one of the more stable constituents of the body and losses of it are not made good.

The line of the iris divides the eye into its anterior and posterior chambers. The anterior chamber, and that part of the posterior chamber that lies between the iris and the lens, is filled with intra-ocular fluid or aqueous humour. This fluid is continually secreted by the epithelium of the ciliary body and drained away into the blood through an opening at the corneo-scleral junction called the canal of Schlemm (see Plate 1).

The aqueous humour is under pressure in the eye and is responsible for the intra-ocular pressure. If the intra-ocular pressure falls seriously, due to loss of aqueous humour, the eye collapses. The chemical constitution of aqueous humour differs in different species but, although these variations reflect to some extent differences in the constitution of the blood plasma, the whole reason for the aqueous differences is not known.

The retina is of neural origin, being directly derived from the neural epithelium of the developing forebrain. Early in development two vesicles, the optic vesicles, grow out one on either side of the forebrain vesicle. Later there is an invagination of the optic vesicles to form the optic cups (Plate 2a). The proximal layer of the optic cup develops to form the pigment epithelium of the retina, while the distal layer becomes the retina proper. Since the original neural tube is formed by an invagination of the surface ectoderm, the surface cells produce its inner lining, and, as a result of the second invagination of the optic vesicles, these cells come to lie on the edge of the retina in contact with the pigment epithelium and so in close association with the choroid. It is from these cells that the light-sensitive visual cells of the retina finally develop so that in the mature eye the visual cells lie on the outer retinal surface turned away from the light, which has to pass through not only the cornea, lens and vitreous, but also through the thickness of the retina before reaching them. In such inverte-brate eyes as those of cephalopods, where there is no double invagina-tion during development, the sensitive cells point towards the light.

The retina consists essentially of four rows of cells of which the outermost, the pigment epithelium, is not directly concerned with photoreception. The pigment epithelium is, however, apparently important for the production of the light-sensitive pigments con-tained in the visual cells. In section it consists of a single layer of six-sided cells firmly attached to the inner surface of the choroid. These cells send processes down between the outer segments of the visual cells and both the cell bodies and their processes contain numerous granules of dark brown pigment. In species in which there is a tapetum the pigment epithelial cells lying over it are not pigmented. In the retina proper the outermost layer of cells is composed of the nuclei of the visual cells and it may be thick in the nocturnal retina, up to ten or twelve rows of cells, or thin in the diurnal retina, a single row only. This outer layer is known as the outer nuclear layer. The outer nuclear layer is separated from the next cell layer by the outer fibre (or plexiform) layer. This consists of the visual cell synapses and of horizontal fibres originating in the horizontal cells lying on the outermost surface of the next nuclear layer. The inner nuclear layer is composed of the horizontal cells, the bipolar cells which are the second neurons of the visual system, the amacrine cells which lie in the inner part of this layer and whose function is not certainly known, and the nuclei of Müller's fibres which are to be found in the central part of the inner nuclear layer. Like that of the outer nuclear layer the thickness of the inner nuclear layer varies greatly in different species. In general it is thin (three to five cells thick) in nocturnal and thick (ten cells thick) in diurnal species. Immediately inside the inner nuclear layer is the inner fibre (or plexiform) layer. This con-tains the synapses between the bipolar and ganglion cells and its thickness varies with that of the inner nuclear layer, being thin where this is thin in the nocturnal retina and thick where the inner nuclear layer is thick in the diurnal retina. Near the inner surface of the retina is the ganglion cell layer. The ganglion cells are the third neurons of the visual system and their axons are the fibres of the

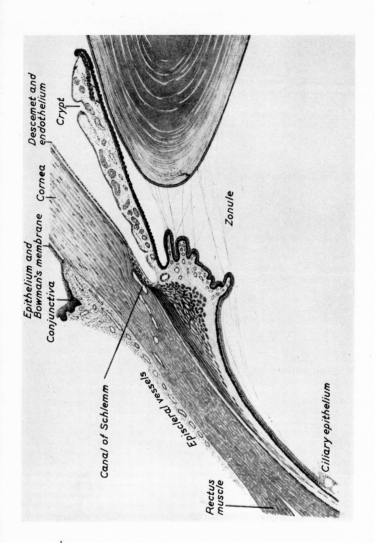

PLATE 1. The corneo-scleral junction. Enlarged section through the area marked *b* in Figure 1 [222].

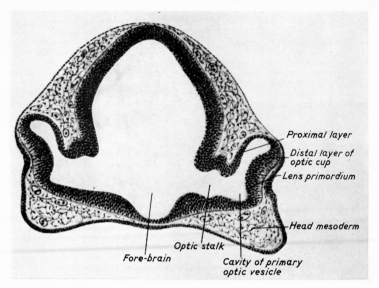

Proximal layer

Distal layer of optic cup

Lens primordium

Head mesoderm

Fore-brain

Optic stalk

Cavity of primary optic vesicle

PLATE 2a. The developing eye. Section through the forebrain of a 5 mm human embryo showing the early formation of the optic cups [222].

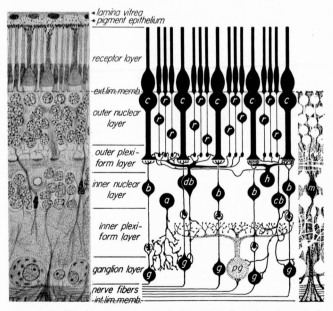

lamina vitrea
pigment epithelium

receptor layer

ext. lim. memb.

outer nuclear layer

outer plexi-form layer

inner nuclear layer

inner plexi-form layer

ganglion layer

nerve fibers

int. lim. memb.

PLATE 2b. The human retina. *Left*: histological section through the human retina (× 500). *Right*: 'wiring diagram' based on specific stains for nerve cells [208].

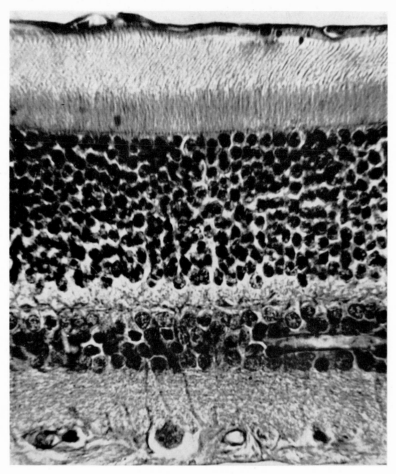

PLATE 3. The nocturnal retina. Section through the central retina of the bush baby, *Galago crassicaudatus*. Note the thick outer nuclear layer and the scarcity of ganglion cells ($\times$ 500).

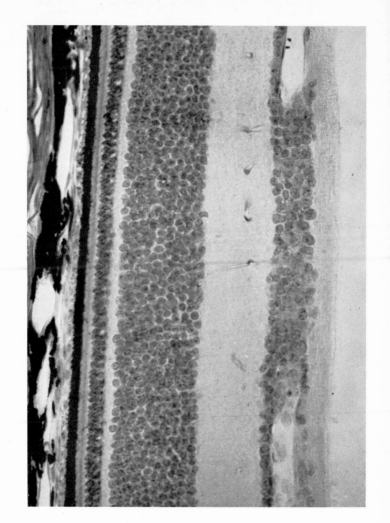

PLATE 4. The diurnal retina. Section through the central retina of the California ground squirrel, *Citellus beecheyi*. Note the thick inner nuclear and ganglion cell layers (× 380).

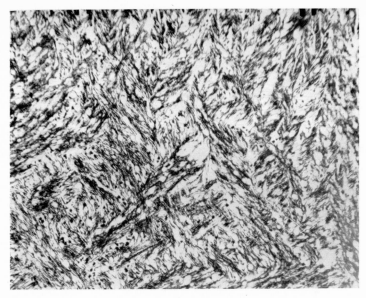

PLATE 5*a*. The optic chiasma. Section through the chiasma of the rabbit showing the crossing of the optic nerve fibres ($\times$ 120).

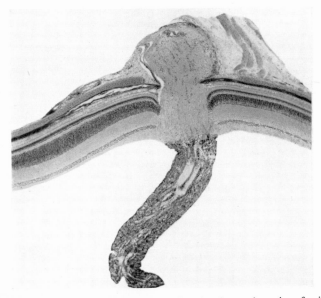

PLATE 5*b*. The conus. Section through a lizard retina at the point of exit of the optic nerve. The conus is attached to the inner surface of the nerve and projects into the vitreous ($\times$ 70).

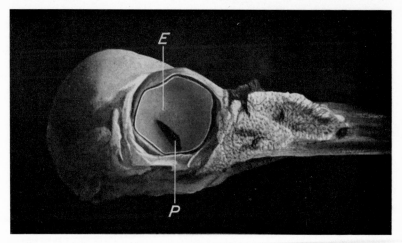

PLATE 6a. The pecten. Dissected right eye of the rook showing the pecten in position [169].

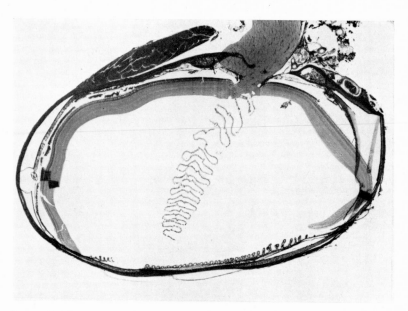

PLATE 6b. The pecten. Section through the eye of a starling showing the pleated structure of the pecten ($\times$ 20).

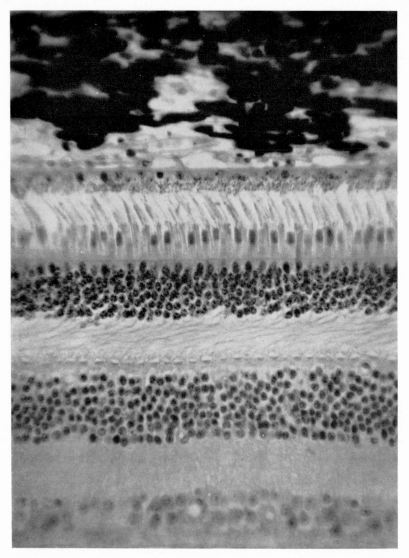

PLATE 7. Rods and cones. Section through the retina of a rhesus monkey showing the two types of visual cell. The larger, more heavily stained cells are the cones, the slender ones in between the rods (× 480).

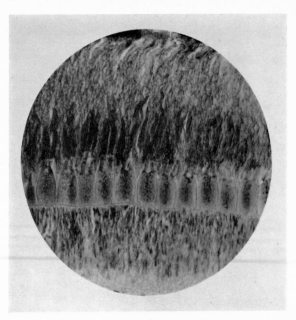

PLATE 8. Twin cones. Section through the visual cell layer of a teleost fish, the pollack. The two pairs of the twin cone are of equal size and are fused along the length of the ellipsoids (× 500).

optic nerve. Once again the number of ganglion cells varies according to whether the retina is a nocturnal or diurnal one. In the nocturnal retina there is usually only one row of ganglion cells which may be widely separated; in the diurnal retina the ganglion cells are much more numerous and the layer may be composed of four to five rows of closely packed cells. The innermost layer of the retina is made up of the axons of the ganglion cells, the optic nerve fibres. Naturally the thickness of this layer depends on the number of ganglion cells present so that it is thick in diurnal retinae and thin in nocturnal ones. Plate 2b shows (on the left) a histological section through the nasal side of the human retina; on the right is a much simplified 'wiring diagram' based on specific nerve stains and giving some idea of the complexity of the nervous connexions within the retina. Plates 3 and 4 are sections through a nocturnal (bush baby) and a diurnal (ground squirrel) retina respectively illustrating the differences just described.

The retinal structures are held together by a system of supporting (glial) fibres usually known as the radial or Müller's fibres. The nuclei of these fibres lie in the centre of the inner nuclear layer and their ramifications run throughout the retina insulating and supporting the true nervous elements. The outer ends of Müller's fibres form a network through the holes in which the visual cells protrude. This is the external limiting membrane and it lies just outside the outer nuclear layer (Plate 2b). The inner ends of the fibres expand into trumpets or pyramids whose bases lie in contact with one another and form an unbroken mosaic, the internal limiting membrane. It has been thought that Müller's fibres were simply supporting and insulating structures but in most species they contain much of the retinal glycogen and may also be of importance for the retinal metabolism.

All the axons of the ganglion cells are gathered up to form the optic nerve. This leaves the eye at the optic disc, or nerve head, pierces the sclera and travels back through the orbit to enter the cranium. Within the cranium the two optic nerves cross through one another (Plate 5a) and continue, as the optic tracts, into the brain. In all the vertebrates, except the mammals, this crossing at the chiasma, is complete, all the fibres from one eye going to the opposite side of the brain. In mammals the crossing, or decussation, is incomplete the extent of it depending on the species. In general, mammals with lateral eyes show a more complete decussation than those with frontal eyes. In rabbits the decussation is almost complete while in cats about two thirds of the fibres cross. In the primates, including man, the proportion of crossed fibres is only one half.

It has already been stated that the visual cells derive their nutrition from the unusually rich blood supply of the choroid. In a few mammalian species the choroid is much underdeveloped and then the visual cells are supplied by the retinal blood vessels which, in these species, extend out to the external limiting membrane. This situation is to be found in the nocturnal flying squirrels and dormouse. The opossum has a relatively impermeable tapetum and here also the visual cells are apparently dependent on the retinal circulation.

Except for the eels in which the retinal capillaries also extend as far as the external limiting membrane, the only animals to have a true retinal circulation are the mammals. The retinal artery enters the eyeball through the optic nerve and branches on the inner retinal surface. In most mammals capillaries extend through the retina to the outer fibre layer. The retinal vessels are, on the whole, poorly developed and less extensive in nocturnal mammals although the bush baby, with an especially rich blood supply, is an exception. The ungulates and carnivores as well as the diurnal primates are particularly well off in this respect. There is no retinal circulation in the monotremes (e.g. the spiny anteater) or, oddly, in the rhinoceros and it is poor in whales and, with the exception of the opossum, in marsupials.

There is no blood supply to the retina in such lower vertebrates as the lampreys, elasmobranch or chondrostean (e.g. sturgeon) fish or, among the reptiles, in turtles or tortoises. All these animals are cold-blooded and, with the exception of turtles and tortoises, nocturnal and presumably the metabolic requirements of their retinae are not great. Holostean (bowrin and garfish) and some teleost fish, amphibia and snakes all have a network of blood vessels in the vitreous on the inner surface of the retina. Most teleosts, however, have a falciform process instead of this network. The falciform process is an invagination of the choroid which enters the posterior chamber alongside the optic nerve and projects into the vitreous as far as the lens. In lizards and those snakes which have good vision there is a highly vascularized conus protruding into the vitreous from the optic nerve head (Plate 5b). The conus is smaller and less well developed in snakes and its framework consists of mesodermal tissue and not of neuroglia as is the case in lizards. Lizards have excellent vision, better than that of any other vertebrates except birds.

In birds there is a specialized structure peculiar to the avian eye and probably homologous with the lizard conus. This is the pecten, a highly vascular pigmented structure, usually pleated but sometimes with vanes, attached to the optic nerve head and standing up in the posterior chamber supported by the highly viscous vitreous body. It is composed almost entirely of blood vessels supported by a light neuroglial network derived from the optic nerve. It is smallest in nocturnal species, larger in seed-eating birds and largest of all in the diurnal predators such as hawks and eagles. The pecten almost certainly provides nutrition and oxygen for the retina although there have been many other theories as to its function (Plates 6a and b).

Not all vertebrates exhibit eye movements but all, except those which have tiny eyes and are virtually blind, such as cave fishes and cave salamanders, have the same set of six extra-ocular muscles. These are arranged in pairs and are the superior and inferior recti, the internal and external recti and the superior and inferior oblique muscles (Figure 3). Contraction of the internal rectus rotates the eye inwards towards the nose, that of the external rectus rotates the eye outwards. The superior rectus turns the eye upwards and inwards and at the same time rotates the right eye in a clockwise and the left eye in a counter-clockwise direction when looked at from in front. The inferior rectus turns the eye downwards and inwards and rotates the right eye counter-clockwise. The superior oblique turns the eyes down and out and rotates the right eye clockwise while the inferior oblique turns the eye upwards and outwards and rotates it counter-clockwise. When the superior rectus and the inferior oblique contract simultaneously the eye is turned vertically upwards, the

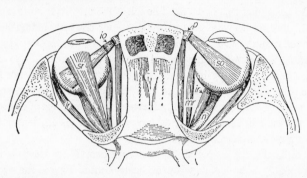

FIG. 3. Oculomotor muscles of man as seen from above in a dissected head. On the left a portion of the superior oblique has been cut away to reveal the inferior oblique; on the right the superior rectus has been removed to show the inferior rectus. *io*, inferior oblique; *ir*, inferior rectus; *lr*, external rectus; *mr*, internal rectus; *n*, optic nerve; *p*, pulley through which the tendon of the superior oblique passes; *so*, superior oblique; *sr*, superior rectus. [208].

other muscular actions cancelling each other out. Eye movements are of two kinds, involuntary and voluntary. Involuntary eye movements are reflex and automatic and their purpose is to keep the visual field as constant as possible during movements of the head and body. Involuntary eye movements are always co-ordinated, that is the two eyes always move in the same sense. If an animal turns sharply to the right, say, then both its eyes will turn to the left, the left eye away from the snout, the right eye towards it. Voluntary eye movements may or may not be co-ordinated. Most lizards and all birds (except the owls) are able to move their eyes independently. In addition, some fishes and the chameleons are able to converge their eyes for binocular vision of a near object. Mammals (and mammals only) show conjugate eye movements; they are quite incapable of voluntarily moving one eye independently of the other. Most fish have only involuntary reflex eye movements. These are mostly in the horizontal plane except in bottom hugging species such as the flat fish and rays. In these the eye movements are up and down and in consequence in them the superior and inferior rectus muscles are more highly developed than the external and internal ones. In fish with mostly horizontal eye movements the external and internal recti are the better developed. Voluntary eye movements are always associated with the presence of a fovea (see Chapter 4) or other retinal area of superior vision. Those fish, all marine and littoral, which possess a fovea are also capable of voluntary convergence on an interesting object in the vicinity. Amphibian eyes do not turn in the orbit at all; these species are only capable of involuntary reflex movements to retract or elevate the eye. Most reptilian species can achieve voluntary eye movements. Turtles, particularly the carnivorous ones, have voluntary lateral movements serving binocular vision. These lateral movements are always co-ordinated but turtles can move the two eyes independently in the vertical direction. Lizards do not have much binocular vision and they can and do move their eyes independently. Independent eye movements reach their highest development in the chameleon which can aim one eye backwards while the other looks straight forwards. This animal continually explores its surroundings using the two eyes independently, but when it sees insect prey it can voluntarily co-ordinate its eye movements for binocular vision. Snakes have little spontaneous ocular mobility and they compensate for this by continual side to side movements of the head. Birds have very big eyes which are a tight fit in the orbit (the owl eye cannot be moved in the orbit even with a pair of pliers!) and so little eye movement even involuntary, and this is replaced by reflex head movements. What movement there is usually is in the horizontal plane and some birds are capable of a slight convergence. The majority of mammals show little voluntary eye movement since they possess no fovea or other specialized retinal area. All the same, mammals prefer to examine external objects binocularly and this usually entails head movements and, in species with lateral eyes like the horse, is restricted to relatively distant objects. Small nocturnal mammals such as bats, small rodents and insectivores, altogether lack eye movements even reflex ones. It is said that among mammals only the monkeys are able to converge; but, of course, those with frontal eyes like the cats will have good binocular vision without convergence. We shall consider binocular vision in more detail in Chapter 13.

2. The Physiology of the Retina

The visual cells of the retina are of two kinds called rods and cones (Plate 7). Fundamentally both are built on the same plan and although it is always possible to tell the two apart when they occur in the same retina, it can sometimes be very difficult to decide whether the visual cells of an unfamiliar species, where all are of the same type, are rods or cones. It may be necessary to take the physiological properties of the retina into account before making a decision.

All visual cells consist of an outer segment making contact with the processes of the pigment epithelium, an inner segment, a nucleus and a synapse. The outer and inner segments lie outside the external limiting membrane and the nucleus inside it in the outer nuclear layer. The synapse is situated in the outer fibre layer. The outer segment is cylindrical or slightly tapering towards the tip and is made up of a stack of ultra-microscopic double membrane discs orientated at right angles to the length of the cell. The inner segment extends from the base of the outer segment (to which it is connected by a modified cilium) to the external limiting membrane. In cones the nucleus usually lies directly beneath this membrane while the rod nuclei are nearly always deeper in the outer nuclear layer and are connected to the inner segment by a fibre resembling an unmyelinated nerve fibre. The distal part of the inner segment contains the ellipsoid which appears to be the most metabolically active part of the visual cell since it is filled with mitochondria. These are more numerous and closely packed in the cones than in the rods. Between the ellipsoid and the nucleus in cones, or between it and the connecting fibre in rods, is the myoid which in some species is highly contractile (see Chapter 6). There is nothing unusual about the nucleus although it is often structurally rather different in the two types, the cones nucleus looking more like that of most vertebrate cells while the rod nucleus is smaller and stains more deeply with nuclear stains.

From the level of the nucleus a fibre usually extends down through the outer nuclear layer to end in a synapse with one or more bipolar cells.

The cone is almost certainly the older and more primitive of the two visual cell types although there are authors who believe the reverse to be true [158]. Cones are associated with diurnal vision and the primitive ancestors of the vertebrate stock were certainly diurnal in habit. The cone outer segment is always slender and, except in the primate fovea, much smaller in diameter than the ellipsoid. It is usually cylindrical but may show a slight taper to the outer tip. In many species amphibia, reptiles and birds the cone contains an oil droplet at the outer end of the ellipsoid. These oil droplets, when present, are coloured (usually yellow but in birds also orange and red) in diurnal species and colourless in nocturnal ones. In fish and reptiles other than snakes some cone inner segments contain a paraboloid, a large oval body composed mainly of glycogen, lying between the ellipsoid and the myoid. The cone nucleus usually lies just below the external limiting membrane although in some types of cone in some species it protrudes through the membrane or may even lie wholly outside it. Occasionally the cone nucleus is to be found deeper in the outer nuclear layer (e.g. in the frog), with the rod nuclei under the external limiting membrane, but this arrangement is not typical. Double cones are widespread among the vertebrates occurring in holostean fish, amphibia, reptiles, birds, one monotreme (the platypus) and marsupials [156, 157], but not in any placental mammal so far investigated. The typical double cone consists of two very unlike cells fused together in the myoid region. The principal member of the pair is like a typical single cone but it never has a paraboloid; the accessory member usually has a large paraboloid but does not have an oil droplet in species where the single cone exhibits one (Figure 4). Double cones are produced late in the development of the retina and appear to be the result of fusion between the accessory cone, which is the first to develop, and a single visual cell which could be a rod [175] or a cone but is more probably a cone. The function of double cones is quite unknown and it is difficult to guess what might be the reason for their production. The outer segments,

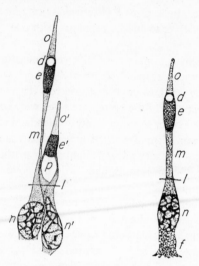

FIG. 4. Cones. Double and single cone from the frog retina showing all the characteristic features. *o*, outer segment; *d*, oil droplet; *e*, ellipsoid; *m*, myoid; *p*, paraboloid; *l*, external limiting membrane; *n*, nucleus; *f*, fibre. × 2800. [208].

nuclei and synapses of the two members are apparently quite separate and all the features of a double cone, such as oil droplet and paraboloid, may also occur in one single cone. Double cones are much more numerous in the retinae of strongly diurnal species. They do not occur in teleost fish, instead there are twin cones where two identical members are fused together along the length of the ellipsoid and myoid (Plate 8). We know even less about twin cones than about double cones although they too seem to be connected with diurnal vision since they are more numerous in surface fish [225], but are apparently excluded from the fovea. Cones ordinarily vary in size according to the part of the retina which they occupy. They are typically thinner and closer packed in the central retina than in the periphery.

The most prominent feature of the rod is the cylindrical outer segment which always has about the same diameter as the ellipsoid.

In many species the outer segment is conspicuously large (Figure 5). Unless they have had a peculiar evolutionary history rods never contain an oil droplet or a paraboloid, nor are double or twin rods to be found. However, in some species, such as nocturnal lizards, including the geckos, and snakes, which have become nocturnal in comparatively recent times the rods look just like cones, both single and double, except for their heavy outer segments. These rods have apparently been transmuted from the cones of diurnal ancestors [203] and paraboloids are present in the accessory members of the double rods. There may even be an oil droplet in the principal member although this is never coloured [190]. In these species too

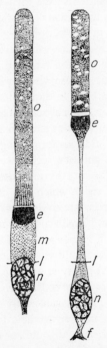

FIG. 5. Rods. Two types of rod from the frog retina. *Right*: the more common red rod; *Left*: green rod. *o*, outer segment; *e*, ellipsoid; *m*, myoid; *l*, external limiting membrane; *n*, nucleus; *f*, fibre. × 1730. [208].

the rod synapse is often a complex one more like that normally typical of cones.

If one looks at the vertebrates as a whole one finds that cones predominate in diurnal retinae and rods in nocturnal ones. In some strongly diurnal species such as the lizards and, among mammals, the squirrels (but not the flying squirrels which are nocturnal) all the visual cells are cones, while in really nocturnal species such as the bush baby the visual cells are all rods. This fact was first discovered by Schultze [176] in the course of a lifetime's study of the comparative anatomy of the vertebrate retina. In consequence he suggested that the rods serve dim-light vision and the cones bright-light vision. And because, in the human retina, the small central area (the fovea) contains only cones and is the region of good colour and form vision, while rods predominate in the periphery where colour and form vision are not so good, Schultze also said that the cones are the organs not only for colour vision but also for good form vision, while the rods serve the achromatic diffuse vision which we experience at night. Our foveal retina is blind in dim lights which is why one has to look at faint light sources, such as some stars, 'out of the corner of one's eye'. We use our central retina and cones for bright-light vision and our peripheral retina and rods for dim-light vision.

When we speak of an animal's seeing well or poorly, or of its being blind in bright lights but having good night vision, we are mixing up two aspects of vision which it is important to keep separate. In fact these two aspects are so different that they are, to some extent, mutually exclusive. Visual acuity, or resolving power, which is the ability to distinguish fine detail, should not be confused with visual sensitivity which is the ability to appreciate small quantities of light as such. Good visual acuity is a property of the cones; high visual sensitivity a property of the rods. Therefore daylight, or cone, vision is characterized by a high visual acuity as well as colour vision while twilight, or rod vision is remarkable for its high sensitivity. The resolving power, or fineness of 'grain', of a retina depends partly on the slenderness of its visual cells, partly on how closely they are packed, but mainly on the number of visual cells finally connected to each optic nerve fibre, since the responses of individual optic nerve fibres constitute the actual messages relayed to the brain. The first two requirements for a high visual acuity are really self-evident. If the images of two point sources of light fall on two visual cells with a relatively unstimulated cell between them, two different nerve fibres will be stimulated and the points recognized as separate. The thinner and nearer together the two cells the closer can the light sources be and still be appreciated as separate. If the light sources are close enough together for their images to stimulate two adjacent cells it is impossible to tell that there are two sources rather than one with a big enough image to cover both cells. Of course this argument would break down if more than one visual cell were ultimately connected to each optic nerve fibre but in the case of the cones, in any case in daylight vision, this does not seem to occur. Although there are many cross-connexions in a cone retina and in spite of the elaboration of the inner nuclear layer and the fact that many inner nuclear cells appear to be connected to each cone by way of its complex synapse, there does appear to be a straight connexion of each cone to an individual ganglion cell and, therefore, to an individual optic nerve fibre. This can be seen in the 'wiring diagram' shown in Plate 2b where each cone makes contact with a midget bipolar (b) and each of these in turn with a midget ganglion cell (g), so that, although apparently under some influence of neighbouring elements by way of various cross-connexions, each cone does seem to have its own 'private line' to the brain. Of course a cone-dominated retina developed to give a fine grain would be useless if the image thrown upon it by the lens system were unsatisfactory. We shall see in Chapter 4 that diurnal eyes have developed a dioptric system designed to throw a large sharp image on the retina.

When we come to the highly sensitive rod retina the picture is very different. Everything possible has been done to increase sensitivity and, on the whole, this has had to be at the expense of acuity. Rods are either slender and close-packed or else have markedly large outer segments. Both modifications result in an increase in the amount of visual pigment (see next chapter) present per unit area of retina and so an increase in its light-trapping power. But the chief means whereby sensitivity is attained is by 'summation'. In a typical rod retina many visual cells (it may be hundreds) are finally connected with each optic nerve fibre. There is summation of the rods on to the bipolar cells and summation of bipolar cells on to ganglion cells. It seems that while a weak response of one rod may not be able to stimulate a bipolar cell to discharge, weak responses from many rods simultaneously will have the desired effect. The threshold (the smallest stimulus to which it can respond) of individual visual cells, whether rods or cones, appear to be much the same [218], but the threshold of a whole rod retina is much lower than that of a whole cone retina and this is mostly due to summation in the rod retina. Although a highly sensitive rod retina, such as that of the bush baby or the conger eel, is usually characterized by a vast number of slender close-packed rods this does not make for a high acuity because hundreds of these rods are connected to each optic nerve fibre of which there are relatively few. The final grain of the retina is, there-fore, determined not by the size and closeness of the individual visual cells but by relatively large groups of them. The increase of sensitivity brought about by summation goes hand in hand with a decrease in acuity, for a high visual acuity, as we have seen, depends on each nerve fibre responding to stimulation of the smallest possible retinal area. This necessary decrease of visual acuity when highly sensitive vision is required is the reason why twilight vision is diffuse and imprecise, as anyone who has tried to read by starlight will realize. The differences in acuity and sensitivity of cone and rod retinae are, therefore, not so much a property of the visual cells them-selves as of the organization of their nervous connexions within the retina. With a few exceptions, for which there are other explanations, cones always do have a 'private line' through to the brain, although they are capable of some summation under certain circumstances, and rods always do show a great deal of summation on to the optic nerve fibres.

Schultze's original formulation was later enlarged and modified by von Kries [122], mostly on the basis of the differences in human day- and night-vision, and called by him the duplicity theory. The duplicity theory states that the sharp coloured vision experienced by man at high illuminations and characteristic of his central retina is due to the reactions of the cones, whereas the diffuse but highly sensitive vision of the peripheral retina at low illuminations is due to the rods. The theory has come in for considerable criticism since von Kries's day, especially from those concerned primarily with human vision, and we have already seen that it is the different nervous organizations of the retina rather than the rods and cones as such which are responsible for the differences between day- and night-vision. However, on the whole, the duplicity theory has stood the test of time and by and large it appears to be true.

When an eye is stimulated by light, certain electrical changes can be recorded both from the retina as a whole and from individual optic nerve fibres. The response of the whole retina takes the form of a series of potential changes which, when recorded, are collectively known as the electroretinogram. The most straightforward way of recording an electroretinogram is to place one electrode on the outer surface of the retina and the other on the inner surface. It is also possible to get a recording if one electrode is placed on the forehead near the eye and the other on the cornea. An electroretinogram can thus be recorded from an intact eye and this is frequently done in man for clinical purposes. When an eye receives a sufficiently intense light stimulus the outer retinal surface becomes first positive and then negative to the inner. When the stimulus is removed there may be a further negative wave which is known as the off-effect. In taking an electroretinogram it is the convention to use the corneal potential change in labelling the sign of each wave so that, according to this convention, the first wave, the a-wave, is negative, the second, the b-wave, is positive and the off-effect, when there is one, is once again positive. Some eyes produce another and much slower positive wave after the b-wave and this slow wave is called the c-wave. Both the a-wave and the off-effect are much more prominent in cone than in rod retinae (Figure 6). In a mixed rod and cone retina, such as that of the frog, the off-effect (and sometimes the a-wave) is much more prominent when the cones are the more active in light adaptation than when the rods are the more active in dark adaptation. It has been found that the amplitude of the b-wave varies directly with the logarithm of the intensity of the stimulating light and that a light of

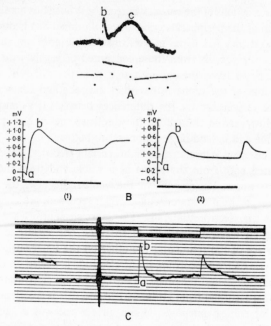

FIG. 6. Different types of electroretinogram. A rod-dominated rabbit eye; dark adapted; one-second stimulus; B, mixed rod and cone frog eye; (1) dark adapted, (2) light adapted; two-second stimulus; C, pure-cone squirrel eye; light adapted; one-second stimulus; calibration, 100 μV.

constant intensity will evoke a larger b-wave in the more sensitive dark-adapted retina than in the less sensitive light-adapted one. The amplitude of the b-wave can, therefore, be used as a measure of retinal sensitivity. This can be a useful method when it is desired to measure changes in retinal sensitivity as, for instance, during dark or light adaptation. The method can also be used for finding the spectral wave-lengths to which the retina is most sensitive. Many people have measured the spectral sensitivity of various animals by this means and we shall consider some of the results in the next chapter.

It is also possible to record the discharge of impulses in individual optic nerve fibres or from individual retinal ganglion cells. Such records can only be made in experimental animals for the technique entails either cutting the eye open or inserting an electrode into the optic nerve. The simplest method was devised by Granit and Svaetichin [94]. They removed the cornea, lens and some of the vitreous from an anaesthetized or decerebrate animal and placed a platinum microelectrode in contact with a ganglion cell on the inner surface of the retina. The nerve impulses discharged from the cell

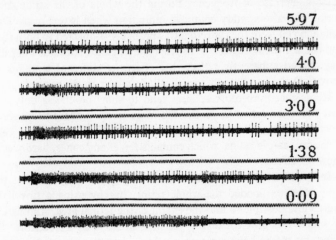

FIG. 7. Ganglion cell discharge. The alteration of the discharge of a spontaneously active ganglion cell from the retina of a dark-adapted cat. The figures on the right give the densities of the neutral filters used in the stimulating light beam [93].

are in the form of rapid potential changes which can be amplified and either displayed on a cathode-ray tube or listened to in a loudspeaker. The sort of record that can be obtained in this way is illustrated in Figure 7 which shows the discharge of a ganglion cell in a dark-adapted cat retina and the way in which the pattern of discharge changed when the intensity of the stimulating light was increased. This ganglion cell, like many others, was spontaneously active in the dark. The effect of the lowest intensity stimulus (filter 5.97) was to slow the discharge somewhat, while there was an increase in frequency again when the light was switched off. When the stimulus was a little more intense (filter 4.0) there was a marked increase of frequency at 'on' and little change at 'off'. A further increase in stimulus intensity (filter 3.09) produced an increased on-effect and a certain amount of inhibition at 'off'. A higher intensity still (filter 1.38) resulted in increased discharges both at 'on' and 'off' while the highest intensity used in this experiment (filter 0.09) caused a very marked increase of frequency during the whole of the stimulation period and a temporary complete inhibition when it was over. This ganglion cell from the cat retina was probably connected to both rods and cones and the changes in its response when the stimulus intensity was altered apparently reflects the effects of different amounts of activity in the two types of visual cell. As a very rough generalization it seems that pure-rod responses tend to show on-effects only and that the more active the cones the more likely is there to be some reaction (either excitation or inhibition) at 'off'. The ganglion cells of the guinea-pig retina, which contains few if any cones, hardly ever show off-effects.

In Granit's [93] experiments, which we have been considering, the light stimulus flooded the whole retina, but by using a tiny light source it is possible to find the extent of the retinal area, stimulation of which will produce discharges in a single optic nerve fibre. By using this method one can get some idea of the fineness of the retinal 'grain'. Quantitative results have been obtained in the frog [16, 102], rabbit [186] and cat [17]. The rabbit and cat both have predominantly rod retinae. In each case the 'receptive field' for a single ganglion cell was found to stretch over about 1 mm^2 of the retinal surface, although in the frog there was some indication that the receptive fields in the central retina were smaller. None of these three retinae has a pure-cone area so that we still do not know how big the receptive fields in a pure-cone retina actually are. In the frog and the cat (the experiments were not tried in the rabbit) stimulation of the retinal area surrounding the receptive field changes the response of the nerve fibre serving the field. Thus, if the normal response of a fibre is at 'on', stimulation just outside its receptive field will inhibit the on-response and substitute an off-response, and vice versa. This inhibitory reaction only occurs in light adaptation, at least in the cat. Receptive fields overlap one another so that not only do the reactions of many visual cells affect each optic nerve fibre, anyway in retinae with plenty of rods, but the reactions of any given visual cell can affect several nerve fibres. This is a consequence of the extreme complexity of the nervous connexions within the retina.

The responses of individual optic nerve fibres recorded by means of Granit's microelectrode technique can also be used to investigate the retinal reactions to stimuli of different colours. By measuring the smallest coloured stimulus required to evoke a discharge it has been found that in a number of retinae different nerve fibres responded differently to changes in wave-length. Thus, if the lowest effective intensities of a series of different coloured stimuli throughout the spectrum were determined for a single ganglion cell it was possible to construct a spectral sensitivity curve for that cell. When a number of such curves for different ganglion cells in a given species were calculated it was often found that there were several different types of curve, indicating that not all parts of the retina responded alike to colour. It was much easier to record different curves for different ganglion cells from retinae which are rich in cones such as those of the frog, snake and tortoise, and it was necessary to work on a light-adapted retina. These findings will be described in more detail and their bearing on colour vision discussed in Chapter 10.

The reactions of a cone retina are much faster than those of a rod retina. This can be seen in Figure 6 where A and C are electroretinograms from the rod-dominated retina of the rabbit and the pure-cone retina of the grey squirrel respectively. The duration of the stimulus was the same in each case (one second) but the record for the squirrel is more spread out (photographed on a more quickly moving film) than that for the rabbit. It is clear that the b-wave in the squirrel is over much sooner than it is in the rabbit. The difference in the speed of response of cone and rod retinae can also be seen if short intermittent stimuli are used. If the rate of flicker is slow the retina responds to each stimulus with a b-wave. As the rate is increased the b-waves get closer and closer together and finally fuse to produce one prolonged positive potential (Figure 8). The frequency at which

c

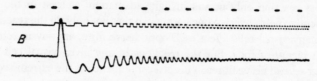

FIG. 8. The response to flicker. The response of the cat electroretinogram to an intermittent light stimulus of increasing frequency [71].

fusion occurs is much lower in a nearly pure-rod retina such as that of the guinea-pig than in a cone retina such as that of the squirrel under the same conditions. The fusion frequency of any species is dependent on the stimulus intensity being higher the greater the intensity. However, using much the same intensity and a light – dark ratio of one-to-one for the flickering stimulus the fusion frequency for the guinea-pig was found to be at about 45 flashes per second [77] and that for a variety of squirrel species at over 100 flashes per second. We shall consider these results again during discussion of the perception of movement (Chapter 9).

3. The Visual Pigments

In the sea urchin, light is able directly to stimulate the radial nerve net [142], but in vertebrates light has no direct effect on the optic nerve. In order for light falling on the eye to affect the discharges in the optic nerve there must be some light-sensitive mediating mechanism. In the vertebrate eye this mechanism consists of photosensitive pigments situated in the outer segments of the visual cells. If a retina containing plenty of rods is removed in the dark room from the eye of a dark-adapted animal and examined immediately under the microscope, the rod outer segments can be seen to be coloured and this colour quickly disappears under the influence of light. It is not possible to see any colour in the cone outer segments by this method. If such a dark-adapted retina is treated with detergent solutions, of which digitonin is the most satisfactory, the pigment can be extracted and brought into solution where its properties can be examined. Visual pigments from a large number of different vertebrates have been studied by this means and all have many properties in common.

All the visual pigments so far investigated are conjugated proteins in which the chromophore group attached to the protein and which is responsible for the colour of the compound is vitamin A aldehyde [15]. When a dark-adapted retina or a visual pigment solution is subjected to light at room temperature the vitamin A aldehyde is finally split off from the protein to appear as a yellow substance early named 'retinene' [197]. Most visual pigments are based on vitamin A_1 and produce vitamin A_1 aldehyde or $retinene_1$ on bleaching, but a number are based on vitamin A_2 and produce vitamin A_2 aldehyde [41] or $retinene_2$ [199]. In the early days it was believed that there were only two rod visual pigments, visual purple, or rhodopsin, based on vitamin A_1 and visual violet, or porphyropsin, based on vitamin A_2, but more recent work has revealed a multiplicity of visual pigments among the vertebrates.

A visual pigment is characterized, not only by whether it contains retinene$_1$ or retinene$_2$, but also by its colour. All the visual pigments are coloured and this means that they do not absorb all wave-lengths of light equally. Most of them absorb more of the green wave-lengths from the middle of the visible spectrum and, in consequence, look red; but some have their maximum absorption in the blue part of the spectrum and so look yellow. When one has an extracted visual pigment in solution it is possible to obtain its density spectrum by measuring the proportion of a selection of wave-lengths taken throughout the spectrum absorbed by the solution. It is, of course, important that these coloured lights should not be intense enough to bleach the solution. Since digitonin extracts of the retina usually contain coloured impurities unrelated to the visual pigments, difference spectra are often measured. The density spectrum of the original coloured solution is measured, the solution is then exposed to light so that it is bleached and the density spectrum measured once again. Since the coloured impurities are not affected by light, the difference between the two curves gives a better picture of the wave-length absorption of the original pigment. In Figure 9 the difference spectra of four visual pigments are shown; these were obtained from (reading from left to right) the tench, the frog, the tench again and the chicken, and the 'positive' parts of the curves are quite a close approximation to the spectrum of the parent pigment. The 'negative' parts indicate that short-wave absorbing (yellow) products were formed on bleaching so that the bleached solutions absorbed more heavily in this part of the spectrum than the original solutions. These pigments can be described by their wave-lengths of maximum absorption as well as by their vitamin. Thus, again reading from left to right the frog pigment is called 502_1, the second tench pigment 533_2 and the chicken pigment 562_1. The absorption characteristics of all known visual pigments are so similar that it has been possible to produce a nomogram [56] from which it is possible to construct the whole curve for any such pigment so long as its maximum density is known.

In Figure 9 two visual pigments are shown for the tench, one with its maximum absorption at 467 mμ, the other at 533 mμ. These

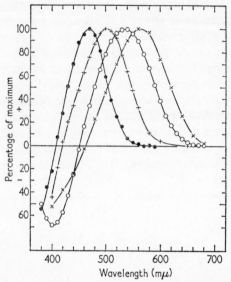

FIG 9. Difference spectra of four visual pigments. Filled circles, pigment 467 from the tench [55]; vertical crosses, pigment 502 from the frog [133]; open circles, pigment 533 from the tench [55]; diagonal crosses, pigment 562 from the chicken [27], [59].

were both extracted by digitonin treatment and appeared in the solution together. They were separated by the method of partial bleaching [55]. After determination of its unbleached density spectrum, the solution was exposed to red light and the spectrum measured again. There was a loss of density around 533 mμ. The solution was then exposed to white light and the red-insensitive component found to have its maximum at 467 mμ. The two components were tested individually by exposing the solutions to a variety of wavelengths and were each found to be homogeneous. This is a very useful technique which can be used satisfactorily if the components of an inhomogeneous solution have their density curves sufficiently far apart to enable one to bleach them separately. Many retinae have been found to contain more than one pigment by this means.

Since the responses of an eye to light are finally dependent on the properties of the visual pigments it contains, one would expect some wave-lengths to be more effective in stimulating the retina than others, the most efficient wave-length being that which is maximally absorbed. In many cases the spectral sensitivity of an eye has been found to correspond to the spectral absorption of its visual pigment and, where this has been measured, to its spectral sensitivity. For instance, the visual pigment extracted from the human eye has its maximum at 497 mμ [52] and this fits well with the spectral sensitivity of the lensless dark-adapted human eye as measured by Dodt and Walther [75] using the *b*-wave of the electroretinogram as the criterion of sensitivity (Figure 10). The human lens is yellow and

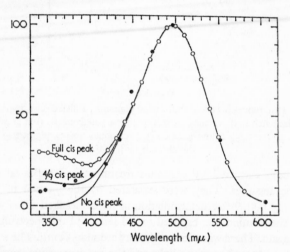

FIG. 10. Comparison between the spectral sensitivity of the human eye and the density spectrum of the mammalian visual pigment. Filled circles, electrotetinographic data for the lensless human eye [75]; open circles, density spectrum of cattle rhodopsin [59].

becomes more so with increasing age, so that the dark-adapted eye with the lens in place is less sensitive to the short wave-lengths absorbed by the lens and the normal spectral-sensitivity curve must be corrected for lens absorption if it is to be compared with the spectral-density curve of the human retinal pigment. A correlation between the spectral sensitivity of the eye and the density spectrum of its visual pigment has also been found for the tench in which Granit [89] obtained the sensitivity curve by electrophysiological means to have its maximum at 533 mμ, where Dartnall [55] found the maximum of the density spectrum of its major visual pigment to lie. Another case in which the agreement is satisfactory is in two species of nocturnal gecko where the spectral sensitivities of *Hemidactylus turcicus* and *Tarentola mauritanica* [76] correspond well with the density spectra of their respective pigments with maxima at 521 and 526 mμ [51]. In the mouse the correlation is also reasonably good. The visual pigment has its density maximum at 498 mμ [36] while the maximum of the spectral-sensitivity curve determined by behaviour experiments is at about 505 mμ [31]. Such good agreement between the spectral-sensitivity curve and the density spectrum of the relevant visual pigment is, however, not common. But this is mainly because the two types of experiment have seldom been done on the same species. Reasonable correlations have been found in the rat, rabbit and cat, although there are some unexplained discrepancies in the rabbit [70] and cat [117].

With the possible exception of 562_1 pigment from the chicken all the visual pigments so far discussed are probably contained in the rods. When we come to consider cone pigments the picture is not nearly so clear cut. If the spectral-sensitivity curve of the human eye is measured in dark adaptation the peak of the curve lies at around 500 mμ in the blue-green. This means that the blue-green part of the spectrum, although under dark-adapted conditions it is not seen as coloured, appears to be the brightest in twilight, or scotopic vision. In daylight, or photopic, vision the spectral sensitivity curve is shifted bodily towards the long wave-lengths and its peak is at 560 mμ in the yellow part of the spectrum. This change of sensitivity was first described by the Czech physiologist Purkinje in 1825 and in his honour it is called the Purkinje shift. There is no Purkinje shift in foveal vision, the sensitivity curve always having its maximum at 560 mμ until the intensity is too low to mediate foveal vision at all. The obvious assumption is that the scotopic curve reflects the sensitivity of the rods and their pigment and that the photopic curve reflects the sensitivity of the cones and theirs. This interpretation is borne out by the fact that a Purkinje shift can often be demonstrated either by behavioural or electro-physiological means in an animal whose retina contains a fair proportion of both rods and cones, and not in one whose retina contains only one or the other. Thus, a Purkinje shift has been shown in the mixed retinae of the cat and frog [68], the tench and carp [89], the pigeon [78] and the chicken [9] by electro-physiological methods and in the starling [1] and pigeon [29] by behavioural methods. No Purkinje shift could be demonstrated in the almost pure-rod retina of the rabbit or in the pure-rod retina of the nocturnal gecko [68] by electro-physiological means, nor could one be found in the mouse [31] by training methods. As one would expect there is also no Purkinje shift in animals with pure-cone retinae. This has been demonstrated by use of the b-wave of the electroretinogram in various diurnal squirrels [184] and in a diurnal gecko [7] and by the microelectrode technique in the tortoise [89].

We have seen that there are several cases of a good correlation between the scotopic spectral-sensitivity curve of an animal and the density spectrum of the visual pigment extracted from its rods. When we come to consider cone pigments the picture is much less easy to interpret. The maximum of the human photopic spectral-sensitivity curve is at 560 mμ and it has, therefore, been assumed that pigment 562_1 (iodopsin) from the chicken retina is a cone pigment [201], for this retina contains many cones. This appears to be all the more probable since the maximum photopic sensitivity of young chicks was found by training experiments to be at 560 mμ although in full-grown birds the maximum was shifted to 580 mμ [111]. It was suggested that this shift could be due to an increase in density of colour in the oil droplets situated in the chicken cones. One difficulty in attributing iodopsin to the cones is that it has never been found in any other retina besides the chicken's although many with plenty of cones have been examined. In the pigeon a second pigment besides the presumptive rod pigment with its maximum at 505 mμ has been obtained. This second pigment has its maximum at 544 mμ and is considered by its discoverer to be a cone pigment [37]. The difficulty is that the maximum of the pigeon's photopic sensitivity curve obtained both by electro-physiological [78, 91]; and by behavioural [29] methods is at 580 mμ and this discrepency of nearly 40 mμ cannot be explained by invoking the filtering effect of the cone oil droplets [37]. It is hard to see how the pigeon's 544_1 pigment can mediate the pigeon's photopic vision. Attempts to obtain unequivocal cone pigments by extracting pure-cone retinae by conventional methods have mostly failed – no photosensitive pigment at all has been extracted. The only exception is in the case of the grey squirrel where minute quantities of a typical visual pigment with maximum density at 502 mμ were removed [58]. But the squirrel's sensitivity curve, using the b-wave of the electroretinogram as the criterion of sensitivity (this animal shows no Purkinje shift) is a complex one apparently mediated by two mechanism, one maximally sensitive at 480 mμ, the other at 535 mμ. Both sensitivity curves are much narrower than the typical density spectrum of a visual pigment [184]. However, when a behavioural method was used in dark adaptation a conventional curve maximal at around 500 mμ was obtained [6]. Spectral sensitivity curves have been obtained from pure-cone retinae in three other species, two lizards [84] and a diurnal gecko [7]. In all three the curves were narrow, as they are in the squirrels. Attempts to extract a pigment from this particular gecko failed completely.

Another method has been used for studying visual pigments besides extracting them. If a small light is shone into the eye a certain amount of it will be reflected back from behind the retina. This reflected light, which has passed twice through the visual cells, returns through the pupil and its intensity can be measured on emergence. As the light passes through the visual cell outer segments with their contained pigment some of it will be absorbed there if the wavelength is right. Thus, if a series of wave-lengths throughout the spectrum is used, less of those which are maximally absorbed will return through the pupil. In the human peripheral retina, which contains pigment 497_1 (a red pigment), more of the blue-green wave-lengths will be absorbed than of the blue or red. The amount of reflexion at each wave-length is measured in the dark-adapted eye where there is a good concentration of pigment; the eye is then light-adapted to remove as much pigment as possible and the measurements repeated. In this way a difference spectrum can be obtained from the living retina. Measurements on laboratory animals such as the cat, guinea-pig and rabbit and on the human peripheral retina have given difference spectra in good agreement with those of the relevant extracted pigments [170, 171, 213, 214, 219]. Difference spectra have also been obtained from the pure-cone retina of the grey squirrel [215] and from the pure-cone human fovea [172]. The grey squirrel pigment had a narrow difference spectrum maximal at 535 mμ and the curve was very similar to that part of the squirrel's spectral sensitivity curve which is also maximal at this wave-length. Evidence of two difference spectra have been obtained from the normal human fovea, one again maximal at about 540 mμ and very like that from the squirrel and a second maximal at about 590 mμ, also narrow. It has been assumed, naturally enough, that these difference spectra describe the density spectra of two cone pigments, one occurring in the squirrel as well as in man. This assumption has not gone unchallenged. No narrow-band photosensitive pigment has ever been extracted from a retina and some workers deny that such pigments exist at all. Instead, the narrow spectral-sensitivity curves obtained from pure-cone retinae are explained by suggesting that the over-all responses of such retinae are due to an interaction between the usual broad-band type of pigment and its breakdown products which are, in this instance, photosensitive. In the case of the grey squirrel, the 502 pigment extracted did show an unusually stable yellow photoproduct with its density maximum at 480 mμ and which was itself photosensitive. The presence of unexpected breakdown products would distort the difference spectra of pigments measured by the reflexion method and might account for the narrow curves obtained from the grey squirrel and the human fovea.

Early in this chapter we saw that all the visual pigments so far extracted are based on either vitamin A$_1$ or vitamin A$_2$, and it used to be thought that there were only two rod pigments, rhodopsin and porphyropsin, absorbing maximally at 500 mμ and 523 mμ respectively, and two cone pigments, iodopsin absorbing maximally at 560 $m\mu$ and based on vitamin A_1 and cyanopsin absorbing maximally at 600 $m\mu$ and based on vitamin A_2. Cyanopsin has never been extracted from a retina but it has been synthesized *in vitro* by combining retinene$_2$ with the iodopsin protein [200]. The retinene$_1$ pigments were thought only to occur in terrestrial animals and marine fish while those with retinene$_2$ were said to be confined to fresh-water species, fish and some amphibia. Where an animal changes its habitat during its life cycle from salt to fresh water (salmon, trout), from fresh to salt water (eel, lamprey) or from fresh water to the land (terrestrial amphibia) its visual pigment was also said to change from the retinene$_1$ to the retinene$_2$ form or vice versa. However, this simple formulation does not altogether fit the facts. To begin with there are many retinene$_1$ pigments ranging in their maxima from 457 $m\mu$ in a nocturnal gecko to 528 $m\mu$ in another nocturnal gecko [51]. The range of the retinene$_2$ pigments is not so wide it stretches from 520 $m\mu$ in the striped mullet [150] to 543 $m\mu$ in the chubb and rudd [60]. It will be seen that the two types of pigment overlap between 520 and 530 $m\mu$ and whether a pigment is based on one vitamin or the other in this region they are indistinguishable in colour. The restriction of retinene$_1$ pigments to terrestrial and marine habitats and of retinene$_2$ pigments to fresh water habitats is widespread but not quite universal. There are rare occurrences of retinene$_2$ pigments in purely marine fish and more common occurrences of retinene$_1$ pigments in fresh-water species. Rudd and chub retinae both contain a retinene$_1$ pigment as well as a retinene$_2$ and, in the rudd at least, the retinene$_1$ pigment may under certain conditions, account for up to 85 per cent of the total visual pigment [60]. The South African clawed toad, *Xenopus laevis*, a species which passes its life in fresh water, also has a small amount of a retinene$_1$ pigment in its rods [57]. A change in the type of pigment associated with a change in habitat during the life cycle often occurs. Thus, the European eel when in the fresh water (yellow eel) form has a mixture of a 523$_2$ and a 502$_1$ pigment. At its second metamorphosis into a silver eel before leaving fresh water for salt on its way to the spawning grounds in the Sargasso sea, the 523$_2$ pigment disappears and is replaced by a yellow retinene$_1$

pigment with its maximum density at 487 mμ. A similar change takes place in the bullfrog [198] and the Pacific tree frog [51] when the aquatic tadpole metamorphoses into the terrestrial adult. But the tadpoles of the European common frog, *Rana temporaria*, the edible frog, *Rana esculenta*, [48] and the toad, *Bufo boreas halophilus*, [51] appear to have retinene$_1$ pigments in spite of their fresh-water habitat, although the original results perhaps indicate a little retinene$_2$ pigment in the tadpoles of the two frogs. Another apparent exception to the rule that fresh-water species have retinene$_2$ pigments was reported in the sea lamprey, *Petromyzon marinus*. Specimens from a population which has been land-locked in the upper Great Lakes of North America and Canada since 1921 were found to possess a retinene$_1$ pigment at 497 mμ and no other [50]. However, these animals were downstream migrants and when *upstream* migrants of another, sexually mature, population taken on their way to their fresh-water spawning grounds were examined a substantially homogeneous retinene$_2$ pigment at about 520 mμ was obtained. These results and those on the eel already mentioned indicate that the change in pigment is not a response to the salinity of the environment but an anticipation of a coming change. The eel pigment changes from a retinene$_2$ to a retinene$_1$ type while the animal is still in fresh water but when it is preparing for its seaward migration, and the same thing apparently occurs in the downstream lamprey migrants. In the lamprey, too, the change in pigment (in this case from retinene$_1$ to retinene$_2$) at sexual maturity seems to take place while it is still in salt water.

The reason for the change from one type of pigment to the other is quite obscure. It does not appear to be necessarily due to differences in diet. The rudd, which is a fresh-water fish, has a mixture of the two types, a retinene$_2$ pigment with maximum density at 543 mμ and a retinene$_1$ pigment at 510 mμ. The proportions of these vary according to the season and can be changed in the laboratory simply by keeping the fish in the dark with no dietary alteration at all. On the whole, the density maxima of the retinene$_2$ pigments are at the longer wave-lengths and the water of lakes and rivers being rather yellow because of dissolved organic matter, the enhanced sensitivity at longer wave-lengths may be advantageous to fresh-water species. When we consider deep-sea fish the situation is somewhat similar. A number of these from depths between 100 and 1,000 fathoms has been examined and found to have pigments absorbing maximally at about 485 mμ [62]. All had an unusually high concentration of pigment in their retinae. Little sunlight penetrates to these depths (and what does is confined to a narrow band centred at 480 mμ) and much of the available light is due to the bioluminescence of various marine organisms. Many bathypelagic fish also have luminous organs of their own. The spectral distribution of the light emitted by such luminescence is maximal at about 480 mμ. In this connexion it is interesting that when the eel undergoes its second metamorphosis its main visual pigment becomes the deep-sea form with its maximum density at 487 mμ. Because silver eels have never been taken from the Atlantic, although it is probable that they migrate from Europe to the Sargasso Sea to spawn, it is assumed that they must travel at great depths and the nature of their visual pigment supports this assumption.

The gecko pigments are unusual in that they are based on retinene$_1$ but, with a very few exceptions, have absorption maxima in the range of the retinene$_2$ pigments, that is from about 516 mμ to 528 mμ. All these pigments come from nocturnal geckos and, as was mentioned in Chapter 2, the rods of nocturnal geckos are thought to have been transmuted in comparatively recent times from the cones of diurnal ancestors. It has been suggested [51] that the gecko rod pigments represent half-way stages between a typical rod pigment at about 500 mμ and an ancestral cone pigment (which might be iodopsin) with its maximal absorption at 560 mμ.

The exact way in which light impinging on a visual pigment situated in the outer segment of a visual cell sets off a discharge of impulses in the retina is not known. The earliest change that has been recorded on stimulation of the retina by light is a steady positive potential at the visual cell level [38, 39]. The leading edge of this potential appears to be identical with the a-wave of the electroretinogram, the latter part of the wave being cut off by the development of the b-wave of opposite sign. This steady potential has been reliably identified as the receptor potential and it is suggested that depolarization at the level of the synapse draws current from the outer parts of the visual cell. Nerve impulses have never been recorded from the outer retina; they appear to originate in the bipolar cells. We have no idea what changes in the visual cell outer segment result in the development of the receptor potential. In solution, light apparently changes the isomeric configuration of the retinene moiety of the visual pigment molecule thereby allowing the retinene to become detached from the protein as a result of subsequent thermal changes [113]. Even if the action of light on the pigment situated in the outer segment is the same as its action in solution, and this is by no means certain, it is not clear what effect an isomeric change in retinene would produce which could initiate a steady positive potential in the visual cell.

4. Adaptations to Diurnal Habit

With the possible exception of the snakes most strictly diurnal vertebrates depend more on vision than on smell, touch or hearing. Blindfold birds cannot alight properly although they will fly if released in the air. They are unable to orientate themselves correctly to the direction and velocity of the wind as do normal birds [20], so that this faculty apparently depends on vision and not on the feel of the air.

The eyes of a strictly diurnal species need not be, and never are, very sensitive since they are not needed for use at twilight illuminations. Diurnal birds roost at sunset and at least one of the ground squirrels does not emerge from its burrow in the morning until the sun is actually shining on the burrow's mouth, nor can it find its way home if released from a trap in the twilight [129]. This insensitivity of the eye is reflected in the structure of the retina for, except among the birds, most purely diurnal species have only cones present. But, however well developed the retina may be with respect to visual acuity, its fine grain would be useless if the retinal image were inadequate. The first requirement for a high acuity is a big image covering as many visual cells as possible, and the first requirement for a big image is a big eye. Since the diameter of the visual cells does not vary greatly throughout the vertebrates it is the absolute rather than the relative size of the eye that matters. Big animals are likely to have big eyes anyway, but small diurnal animals tend to have eyes which are relatively very large. This is particularly true of the birds whose eyes are relatively enormous, as big as the head can accommodate. The two eyes of a bird may take up so much room that they are practically touching in the midline of the head and one can be stimulated by a light shining right through the other [128]. Diurnal birds' eyes do not look so very big on casual inspection from a distance because the cornea is relatively small and so is the lid opening, but anyone dissecting out such an eye is liable to get quite a surprise. When, for anatomical reasons, the eye can get no bigger the posterior chamber is often much enlarged compared with the anterior chamber (Plate 9). Where this occurs, the lens becomes flattened in order to increase its focal length because the retina is now farther from it. This flattening of the lens with the concomitant increased 'throw' results in an enlargement of the retinal image. It also results in a decreased brightness of the image, but this does not matter in a diurnal eye which always receives plenty of light under its normal working conditions. In diurnal fish (Figure 2) where the refractive index of the lens is unusually high to compensate for the physiological lack of a cornea, the image formed is broad anyway and so the posterior chamber has not been increased in depth; on the contrary, the eye is flattened and so takes up less room in the head. Since the diurnal eye works at high illuminations the pupil can be relatively small, and this is of advantage for visual acuity because it helps to cut down the spherical aberration of the less optically perfect lens edges. Not only is the pupil small but it shows much less change in size with changes in the ambient illumination. Although birds have extremely active pupils the bird iris is relatively insensitive to light and it has been suggested that the bird pupil is under voluntary control; birds are unique in that the iris muscles are striated. The bird (in any case the parrot) pupil contracts as an interesting object approaches the eye, but it is not known whether this is a reflex contraction linked to accommodation as it is in man. In man the accommodation, pupil contraction and convergence reflexes are linked so that there is always convergence and pupil contraction when the eye accommodates on near objects; birds have little eye movement, although some are said to be capable of a slight convergence. There is no convergence on an approaching object in the parrot.

The diurnal retina and the ways in which it differs from a nocturnal one have already been discussed in Chapters 1 and 2 (see Plates 3 and 4). The diurnal retina usually shows a preponderance of cones and sometimes does not contain rods at all. In a comparison of the retinae of birds of different habits it was found that the more diurnal species, in this case the fulmar petrel and the house sparrow, had more cones and less convergence of visual cells on to the ganglion cells than the Manx shearwater, which is unusual among birds in being active both by day and night [131]. Pure-cone retinae are found in diurnal reptiles and, among mammals, in the diurnal Sciuridae, that is the tree and ground squirrels, chipmunks, prairie dogs and marmots; the flying squirrels are nocturnal and are said to have a nearly pure-rod retina. The only other strictly diurnal mammals known are the agouchis, South American rodents related to the cavies. These animals are suspected of having colour vision but their retinae have never been examined. Diurnal birds have mixed retinae with many more cones than rods, but diurnal fish actually have more rods than cones although here the rods are tiny. Except in certain specialized areas which we shall be considering below, the cones are thicker than the rods and so fewer can be accommodated in a given retinal area. This means fewer visual cell nuclei and, in consequence, a thinner outer nuclear layer which may be anything from one (snakes) or two (turtles, squirrels) to several (lizards, birds) cells thick. Because there are fewer visual cells and so fewer synapses to accommodate the outer fibre layer is also thin in diurnal retinae. Perhaps the most striking thing about the diurnal (and especially the pure-cone) retina is the great thickness of the inner nuclear layer. Of course one would expect a good number of bipolar cells if each visual cell is to have its 'private line' to the optic nerve, but the number of cells in the inner nuclear layer of a diurnal retina is much more than would satisfy this requirement. It is not certain whether there are more bipolar cells than there are visual cells, but there is certainly a great increase in the number of horizontal and amacrine cells. The function of these 'associational' cells is not exactly known, but they apparently improve the detail of the visual image by enhancing contrast phenomena. Visual acuity in man is better than can be explained on the basis merely of the number and dimensions of the foveal cones and it seems that this is achieved by means of a balance of excitation and inhibition at the inner nuclear level reinforced by continual minute eye movements. If the retinal image is stabilized so that eye movements do not produce image movements over the retina, visual acuity is seriously impaired, indeed all detail in the

D

visual field can disappear. In a pure-cone retina the number of ganglion cells may equal the number of visual cells, at least in specialized areas, and the inner and optic nerve fibre layers are always thick. In these retinae too the processes of the pigment epithelium, which extend inwards to the level of the cone ellipsoid, are full of pigment so that each outer segment is optically isolated from its neighbours. This pigment does not alter its position in response to changes in the external illumination (see Chapter 6).

All diurnal retinae have a specialized area of one shape or another where inner nuclear and ganglion cell layers are thicker than in the rest of the retina. This specialized area is known as the *area centralis* although it is not always centrally placed. If the retina is a mixed one, as in birds, the rods are absent from this area and the cones may be more slender and longer. Where the cones are thinner more are packed into a given space and the thickness of the outer nuclear layer is thereby increased. In those retinae which are the most highly developed for visual acuity the *area centralis* contains a pit or depression known as the *fovea centralis*. Here the cells of the inner retina are displaced sideways making a deeper (Plate 10a) or more shallow (Plate 10b) pit with steeper or more gradual slopes at its edges. In mammals, where the retina is vascularized, blood vessels are excluded from the vicinity of the fovea. It is usually believed that the foveal pit is designed to facilitate the passage of light on to the cones by thinning the retina in front of them, but there have been other theories as to the function of the foveal depression. One theory [205] suggests that the actual shape of the fovea produces a slight magnification of the retinal image owing to the fact that the refractive index of the retina is higher than that of the vitreous [192, 193]. Another [162] points out that a deep fovea will distort an image that does not lie on its centre and that this might serve as a stimulus for correct fixation. Foveae are only present in man and the primates among mammals and even here they are not very highly developed. Some people [206] believe they are degenerate. Foveae occur in such sharp-sighted species as lizards and some teleost fish but, with the possible exception of lizards, they are most highly developed in birds. Most birds have their eyes placed laterally in the head and their foveae placed centrally in the retina so that their most acute vision will be to the side. However, many birds (hawks, eagles, humming birds, bitterns and various passerine species including swallows) which are especially well-equipped visually, and particularly those which hunt on the wing and need a good distance judgement, have a second fovea [44] in a posterior temporal position which can be used in conjunction with the other eye for binocular vision. This lateral fovea is seldom as well developed as the central one. In some birds, both with and without foveae, the *area centralis* is a ribbon-like formation running across the retina in a roughly horizontal direction. In the lapwing, oyster-catcher, coot, snipe and herring-gull it has been shown that, although the position of the bill is very variable between these species, when the head is carried in its normal position during life this special area, as well as the semi-circular canal, is always horizontal [80]. This finding suggests a visual aid to giving the bird a plane of reference in relation to the horizon. Such a ribbon-like central area has never been found in forest inhabitants or birds of prey but mainly in birds of the open spaces. It has been suggested that it may be of importance in navigation [159].

An *area centralis* is very common in teleost fish and several of these also have a fovea from which double cones are excluded. The teleost fovea is usually laterally placed in the temporal retina and, since fish eyes tend to protrude from the head, this will give its owner foveal binocular vision straight ahead. There is no fovea in any amphibian or, among the reptiles, in crocodiles and alligators or most turtles, although these all have an *area centralis* which, however, contains rods as well as cones. Diurnal lizards have superb foveae perhaps as good as those of birds, but most snakes have none. Although mostly diurnal, snakes have poor visual acuity owing to their very small eyes and very big cones. Two snakes only have been positively shown to possess a fovea, the East Indian long-nosed tree snake and the African bird snake. In these the eyes are lateral as in all snakes and the fovea is in the temporal retina. There is a special forward prolongation of the pupil making it keyholed in shape. A line through the fovea and the centre of the lens passes through the pupil prolongation and along a groove in the cheek in front of the eye, thus giving forward binocular vision. It is significant that the East Indian snake is agreed to have the best sight and distance judgement of any snake in the world.

The thinning of the foveal cones enhances visual acuity by packing more visual cells into a given space on the retina. Their increase in length, which especially affects the outer segments, has two further advantages. The retinal image is focused on to the visual cell outer segments, but the exact position along the length of the outer segment is immaterial. The longer the outer segments the more latitude there is in positioning the image. Therefore, if the outer segments are long, accommodation need not be so precise. For the same reason long outer segments will diminish the effects of chromatic aberration.

There is no retinal tissue at the site of entry of the optic nerve into the eye, and the nerve-head, therefore, produces a blind spot in the visual field. Where the optic nerve is thin (and this is only in predominantly rod eyes with inferior visual acuity) the blind spot is unimportant and where the eyes are frontally placed and the visual fields overlap, as in our own case, one eye fills in the blind spot of the other. But in diurnal animals the optic nerve is big because of the increased number of ganglion cells and if the eyes are lateral the blind spot could be dangerous. In animals with lateral eyes and big optic nerves this situation is dealt with by flattening the nerve-head into a ribbon and sometimes by moving it out of the way. In diurnal birds and fish the nerve-head is flattened and in birds it is tucked away under the pecten so that there is only one blind area instead of two. In the diurnal squirrels the nerve-head is also flattened and, in addition, it is moved into the upper part of the retina leaving the upper visual field (all images are inverted by the eye's optical system) uninterrupted. It is from the sky that most squirrel species can expect their predators and this arrangement gives them an unimpaired view of it.

All diurnal eyes have some sort of intra-ocular colour filter, usually yellow but sometimes orange and red as well. These take several forms from the yellow corneae of some diurnal fish to the coloured oil droplets in the cones of lizards, turtles and birds. The oldest kind of colour filter appears to be a yellow lens, for this is the type present in lampreys. But the possession of a yellow lens does not necessarily mean that a species is primitive. Coloration of the lens seems to be the easiest way of developing an intra-ocular filter if the other types, and particularly the coloured oil droplets, have been lost during a period of ancestral nocturnality. Yellow lenses, which are considered to be a secondary development, are to be found in snakes, some diurnal geckos and the diurnal squirrels. Apart from other considerations there are ocular features in snakes which suggest that, in developing from lizard ancestors, they went through a nocturnal phase during which the eyes became much degenerated [207]. When the snakes reverted to diurnal habits the eyes had to be redeveloped to a great extent. During the period of nocturnality the visual cells are thought to have lost the coloured oil droplets typical of lizards and these, once lost, cannot be renewed. A yellow lens developed as a substitute. The same thing seems to have happened in some diurnal geckos. Nocturnal geckos on the whole do not have oil droplets and at least one genus of diurnal gecko from the Indian Ocean islands, *Phelsuma*, has only a few colourless oil droplets but a yellow lens instead. The lack of oil droplets in the squirrel retina together with the yellow lens suggests to at least one authority [208] that these species have become secondarily diurnal. The human lens is also yellow but this appears to be, as it were, accidental. The colour increases steadily in density during life and the pigment is melanin, apparently formed by the interaction of protein breakdown products which are produced during ageing of the lens. The chemistry of the pigment of the yellow lenses of other species is not known, but the pigment is not melanin. The yellow colour of the human lens may be incidental but it is none the less useful in diurnal vision. Another intra-ocular colour filter is the macular pigmentation of man and the primates. In these species the inner layers of the retina around the fovea are coloured yellow by a pigment which may be xanthophyll, although this has been questioned. This area of the retina is known as the *macula lutea* or yellow spot; it is centred on the fovea but stretches somewhat beyond it. Coloured oil droplets situated at the outer end of the cone inner segment are a feature of frogs (the only diurnal amphibia) where they are usually yellow although some are colourless, lizards where they are also yellow and turtles and birds where they are red, orange and yellow. Red and orange droplets are not present in the bird fovea where all are yellow. In nocturnal birds the oil droplets are colourless. Coloured oil droplets are also present in the cones of marsupials [156, 157].

In earlier times it was thought that the oil droplets of the bird retina were blue and green as well as red, orange and yellow, but this was due to defective microscope lenses, and with the advent of apochromatic lenses the true situation was realized. One of the theories of colour vision is based on this misconception of oil droplet colours in birds and some of its proponents even went so far as to assert that there are probably coloured oil droplets in the cones of the human fovea [168]. In actual fact the theory will not do at all even for the species which undoubtedly have the coloured droplets. Lizards have been shown to have colour vision by behaviour experiments [196], but they have only yellow oil droplets. In diurnal birds, which are also known to have colour vision as good as ours, the only oil droplets in the fovea are the yellow ones. In any case, a hue discrimination such as the bird's [125] could not be mediated by filters confined to the long-wave half of the spectrum. Further, newly hatched chicks exhibit colour vision [109] but at this age their oil droplets are not pigmented.

The real function of the coloured oil droplets appears to be quite different. As we have seen, all diurnal species have yellow filters of one sort or another and it has been suggested [209] that these, by cutting off the shortest wave part of the spectrum, minimize the effects of chromatic aberration. They can also reduce the glare caused by scattering of the short waves by the atmosphere and enhance contrast especially among the green hues which are so prevalent in natural surroundings. It is further suggested that the red oil droplets of birds serve to eliminate the Rayleigh scattering which occurs at sunrise and sunset. There is some support for this idea in the fact that early risers among birds (e.g. song birds) have more red droplets than later risers such as hawks and these again have more than the crepuscular swifts and swallows. This explanation will not account for the red oil droplets of turtles. These animals, however, have to contend with glare over the water and here both their red and their yellow filters could be helpful, as has been discovered by the United States navy [208]. The kingfisher, which also experiences glare over water, has a higher percentage of red oil droplets than any bird so far examined.

Only eyes adapted for use in bright light can afford coloured filters. Yellow and red filters may do much in the way of sharpening the retinal image by cutting down glare and chromatic aberration but they also entail a considerable loss in the amount of light which reaches the outer segments of the visual cells. This does not matter to a diurnal eye but would be a great handicap to a nocturnal one which needs all the light it can get. Nocturnal eyes never have colour filters. Where diurnal and nocturnal species are closely related, as in the geckos, birds and squirrels, the lens or oil droplets, as the case may be, are always colourless in the nocturnal ones.

5. Adaptations to Nocturnal Habit

The nocturnal habit is always a secondary adaptation. Animals took to the dark when competition for space and food became too intense, or to find refuge from diurnal predators. The predators too have often followed their prey into the night so that, although most strictly nocturnal species are those which are preyed upon, there are also plenty of nocturnal predators. On the whole, the predators have retained reasonably good vision, but many nocturnal species, especially the small mammals, have sacrificed all visual capacities except sensitivity. These animals have come, therefore, to depend much more on smell, hearing and touch than on vision. Mostly they are vegetarian, feeding on foliage or heads of grain for they are, in general, incapable of finding individual seeds or catching living prey. Where a species does live on insect food it is caught in bulk as the anteater does with its sticky tongue. The dependence of strictly nocturnal animals on senses other than vision can be seen in certain strains of rats and mice which suffer from an inherited degeneration of the retina, leading to complete blindness soon after the eyes open in the young. Such animals cannot be distinguished from their normal companions by observing their behaviour under daylight conditions in the laboratory and they do not appear to suffer from any particular disability compared with normally sighted rats and mice. But anyone can recognize a blind kitten from its behaviour.

There are other lightless habitats besides the hours of darkness and some species have retreated to these for protection. There are the dark depths of the sea, under the earth, caves and the bottoms of muddy rivers, and the inhabitants of these places also show ocular adaptations. Mostly they have given up the struggle for vision and have much reduced eyes which are virtually useless. In the Mexican cave fish, *Anoptichthys jordani*, the young fish are hatched with complete small eyes which, however, have no circulation. As the fish grows, the eyes become covered with layers of skin, the lens and pupil disappear and the retina degenerates. In adult fish all that is left is a circle of pigment lying in a recognizable orbit [123]. The other cave species, all either fish or salamanders, also have completely degenerate eyes, although it is not known whether the regression which occurs in *Anoptichthys* represents the usual course of events. Burrowing animals, such as the moles and the fossorial reptiles, have retained enough of an eye to tell light from dark. Abyssal fish, on the other hand, have enormous, highly sensitive eyes well adapted for use in an environment lit by luminescent organisms as well as by their own light-producing organs.

The first essential for a useful nocturnal eye is that it should collect as much light as possible. A big eye with no other modification does not fulfil this requirement, what is needed is a big pupil. But a big pupil entails a big lens if the spherical aberration of the lens periphery is not to become a problem, and these changes lead to a proportionate increase in the size of the cornea as well as of the anterior chamber. The increased size of the lens will increase its focal length so that its curvature (and often that of the cornea as well) has to be increased to bring the focused image back on to the retina. The increase in lens curvature produces a smaller image but a brighter one. In most nocturnal predators, the cat for instance, the whole eye is then enlarged to increase the size of the image without losing any of its brightness, but in strictly nocturnal preyed-upon species like the small rodents the eye is not enlarged and its owner's visual acuity is very poor indeed. Whereas in a diurnal bird with a fovea, such as the homing pigeon, two lines whose retinal images are less than 1 μ

FIG. 11. Nocturnal eyes. The general structure of the eye in three nocturnal species. Note the large lens and cornea. [208].

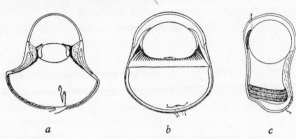

a   *b*   *c*

FIG. 12. Tubular eyes. Characteristic of nocturnal animals with better vision. An adaptation when there is no room in the head to enlarge the eye further. (*a*) owl; (*b*) bush baby; (*c*) deep-sea fish. [208].

apart can be recognized as separate, in the rat the separation of the retinal images has to be over 20 μ. In the human fovea the equivalent distance is 1.89 μ. The nocturnal eye, then, tends to have a large cornea, a large lens which is often nearly spherical, a large pupil and, as a consequence, a large anterior chamber (Figure 11). In strictly nocturnal species with poor vision the eyes are small, but in the better-sighted nocturnal species the eyes tend to become as big as the head can accommodate and they often develop a tubular shape (Figure 12). This occurs where there is not enough space for the whole eyeball to enlarge and instead the depth of the posterior chamber is increased but not the retinal area. The relatively small retinal area does not matter so much because the bright image, although larger than in a small eye, is relatively small too. Tubular eyes are always enormous as in the owl, the bush baby and most deep-sea fish, are frontally placed and are unable to turn in the orbit. To compensate for the lack of eye movement the head usually has a tremendous capacity for rotation; the owl can turns its head through at least 270 degrees, but fish, of course, have to turn the whole body. Nocturnal species with small eyes and poor vision also exhibit little or no eye movement. This is not because there is no room for the eye to turn in the orbit but because with no central area and a spherical lens there is no need for eye movements. With this type of lens, a concentric retina and a large cornea the retinal image is equally good whatever the direction of the external object.

The nocturnal retina is always dominated by rods, but only exceptionally, as in the bush baby, the bats, most elasmobranch fish and the nocturnal snakes and lizards, are there no cones present at all. Nocturnal eyes which are also useful by day, those of the cat and owl for instance, have quite a large number of cones, but those of more strictly nocturnal species which normally never emerge after sunrise (rats, mice and many other small rodents) have so few cones that it is probable that they do not affect vision at all. Such cones as are present are so far apart that they could not provide a reasonable visual acuity even if each has its own single connexion to an individual ganglion cell. It is not know whether this does occur in such retinae. Generally in nocturnal retinae there is an enormous number of long, slender, closely-packed rods showing a great deal of summation on to the bipolar cells, many of which are, in turn, connected to each ganglion cell. There may be several thousand rods ultimately linked to each optic nerve fibre. Therefore in sections of a nocturnal retina we have a thick outer nuclear layer, an inner nuclear layer, which is much thinner, and comparatively few ganglion cells widely separated in a single row. The optic nerve fibre layer is, of course, also very thin (Plate 3). The retina is extremely sensitive and the visual acuity very poor. A retina which should be very sensitive indeed has been described in the abyssal fish, *Bathylagus benedicti*, [194]. In this pure-rod retina the visual cells are, as usual, thin and close-packed, but they are arranged in three rows one outside the other so that three times the normal number of rods can be accommodated. The outer nuclear layer is fourteen cells thick and the inner nuclear layer only two cells thick with, as usual, larger cells much farther apart. There are relatively few ganglion cells. This fish has a temporal fovea where there are six rows of rods instead of the three present in the rest of the retina [195]. There is no increase in the numbers of bipolar and ganglion cells in the region of the fovea, so this must represent a development for increasing sensitivity rather than acuity.

Another deep-sea fish, *Stomias boa ferox*, has a similar type of retina in which there are also only rods, these being arranged in two rows one behind the other [144].

We have already seen that nocturnal eyes which are also used in daylight usually have a respectable number of cones but one type of pure-rod retina has preserved its visual acuity in another way. In the nocturnal geckos all the cones of their diurnal lizard ancestors have been transmuted into rods but in this retina there is much less summation than is usual in nocturnal species. Plate 11 shows a section through the central retina of one of the nocturnal geckos, *Hemidactylus turcicus*, and it can be seen that the number of visual cells is very nearly the same as the number of ganglion cells. Also there appears to be no summation of rods on to bipolar cells. In addition, the rod synapses of this retina are somewhat complex and more reminiscent of the usual cone synapse. It is likely that each rod is connected to more than one bipolar cell. These little lizards have a visual acuity high enough to enable them to catch flying insects by day, but they also become as sensitive as a cat at low illuminations [76]. This high sensitivity can be partly accounted for by the optical structure of the eye [182], but must also be to some extent due to the large amount of visual pigment contained in the massive rod outer segments [61].

If a nocturnal animal wishes, like the cat, to emerge during the day and perhaps bask in the sun it needs some protection for its highly sensitive retina. This protection is provided by the pupil which contracts to the smallest possible size in bright light. But a circular pupil can never close completely and in many nocturnal eyes the pupil, which is round when dilated, contracts to a vertical slit. In the cat the edges of the slit meet along most of its length leaving two minute holes, one at each end, which let in little light but provide pinhole images on the retina. Even this much light can be cut off by partial closure of the lids. A much more elaborate arrangement occurs in many of the nocturnal geckos. Here the pupil is also round when dilated and a vertical slit when contracted, but there is a series of four notches on each edge of the iris. These notches are exactly opposite one another so that when the pupil is closed four tiny holes are left along its length. These holes provide pinhole apertures which form a series of superimposed sharp images on the retina without letting in too much light. Strictly nocturnal mammals have round pupils for they never expose their retinae to bright light by appearing during

the daylight hours; being warm-blooded they are relatively independent of the warmth of the sun. Among the mammals only the small
cats and the dormouse have a vertical slit pupil. Many ungulates have
pupils in the form of horizontal ovals, which, however, never close
completely. The ungulates are not truly nocturnal in habit. Most
terrestrial reptiles like to bask sometimes and those of them which
are nocturnal nearly all have vertically slit pupils; some very secretive burrowers among the snakes are an exception. Diurnal reptile
species have round pupils. There are many bizarre shapes of pupil
among the amphibia but the truly nocturnal species have slit pupils.
Slit pupils may also be seen in some elasmobranch fish which like to
bask at the surface or in shallow water. The rays, which also often
bask, may have slit pupils or, in some species, an operculum. This is a
sort of lobe of the upper iris which can expand and fill the pupil under
the action of light. An analogous structure is often present in whales
and also in the hyrax, while many ungulates have *corpora nigra*. These
are serrated extensions of the iris both above and below the pupil,
which apparently shield the retina from glare either directly from the
sky or reflected upwards from the ground. All birds have round pupils
whether they are nocturnal or diurnal, the black skimmer, a nocturnal
seabird from North America, being the only known exception.

A device for increasing the sensitivity of the eye is the tapetum, a
reflecting structure situated behind the visual cells. Where there is a
tapetum, light that has passed through the visual cells is reflected
back so that it passes through them a second time instead of being
absorbed by the black choroidal pigment. The light thus has two
chances of stimulating the visual cells instead of only one chance. It
is the tapetum which is responsible for the 'eyeshine' of cats and dogs.
A tapetum is never present in a truly diurnal eye for it must always
interfere with visual acuity by blurring the image, but it can make a
useful addition to sensitivity. It has been found that the cat, which
has an extremely efficient tapetum, can, when dark-adapted, recognize a light too dim for an equally dark-adapted human observer to
see. The difference is apparently due to the cat's tapetum [98]. There
are several types of tapetum which are either situated on the inner
surface of the choroid or in the processes of the cells of the pigment

epithelium. In ungulates, some marsupials, elephants and whales the tapetum is made up of tendinous fibres on the inner surface of the choroid. These fibres glisten and reflect the light just like a piece of fresh tendon. In other mammals, the nocturnal prosimians, the carnivora and seals, the tapetum is still on the inner surface of the choroid but it is cellular, composed of a very regular array of rectangular cells put together rather like the bricks in a wall (Plate 12). The reflected colours are an interference phenomenon and the over-all effect is usually yellow or green. The bush baby has an extremely vivid yellow eyeshine which is due to a tapetum. The bush baby tapetum is made up of cells packed with pure crystalline riboflavin lying on the inner surface of the choroid. Riboflavin fluoresces blue-green in ultra-violet light and it has been suggested that it enables the bush baby, which has an exceptionally sensitive eye, to utilize the short wave-lengths, to which it is relatively insensitive, by turning them into longer wave-lengths nearer the point of maximal absorption of its visual pigment. However, this seems not be the case for no ultra-violet light reaches the bush baby retina; it is all absorbed in the ocular media. The bush baby tapetum seems just to be an unusually effective mirror. That part of the pigment epithelium which overlies a choroidal tapetum of either type is always devoid of pigment so that there is no interference with the back reflection of the light.

Some fish have a fibrous tapetum while others have a special type situated in the processes of the pigment epithelium. This 'retinal' tapetum is found in many of the species inhabiting the very turbid waters of Lake Balaton in Hungary. In the retinal tapetum of teleost fish the processes of the pigment epithelial cells are packed with crystals of guanin, a purine related to uric acid which gives the silvery appearance to the scales of many fish. This type of tapetum is occlusible in light adaptation, for under these conditions the dark epithelial pigment migrates inwards towards the external limiting membrane breaking up the guanin layer and destroying its effectiveness as a mirror (see Chapter 6). Elasmobranch fish also have a guanin tapetum but in these species it is situated in the choroid. It was thought at one time that this tapetum was also occlusible by movements of the choroid pigment, but more recent work [155] on the dogfish has shown that, at least in this species, there is no movement of choroidal pigment in response to illumination. It was found that the ventral tapetum was permanently occluded while the dorsal tapetum was permanently exposed. It has been suggested that the dark ventral retina receiving light from above has a higher acuity, while the refecting tapetum increases sensitivity to the much dimmer light coming from below.

The processes whereby an eye becomes progressively more sensitive when taken from the light into the dark are collectively known as dark adaptation. Both rod and cone retinae show dark adaptation, that of the former being slower but much more extensive. Dark adaptation of a pure-cone retina is complete in a few minutes but the increase in sensitivity is not very great [7, 181]. Rod dark adaptation is a great deal slower, taking as much as two hours in the rabbit and even longer in the albino rat [69], but the increase in sensitivity is very much more. In a pure-rod, or nearly pure-rod retina the sensitivity can increase a million times or more, while a pure-cone retina only becomes about a thousand times more sensitive during a stay in complete darkness. The dark adaptation of a mixed retina takes place in two stages; there is an early increase of sensitivity which tails off after a few minutes and a later, much greater increase which also gets slower as time goes on. There is good evidence that the early part of the dark adaptation of a mixed retina is mainly due to the cones and the later part to the rods.

The course of dark adaptation has been studied in several species with all types of retina by finding the light intensity required to produce a standard electroretinographic response after lengthening periods in the dark. This method has been used to follow the course of the dark adaptation of the pure-cone retinae of the grey squirrel [181] and the diurnal gecko, *Phelsuma*, [7] the pure- or nearly pure-rod retinae of the nocturnal gecko, *Hemidactylus*, [72], the rat [69] and the rabbit [82] or the mixed retinae of the cat [82] and frog [73]. An inenious behavioural method has been used for tracing dark adaptation in the pigeon [28], the starling [1] and the American robin. The bird is trained to peck one key if it can see a light source and a second key if the light is invisible. In this way it is possible to assess the least light intensity recognizable by the bird after any given period in the dark. Using this method it was found that the starling's eye is less sensitive than the pigeon's when dark-adapted and this is not surprising because, although rods are present, a large part of the starling retina is pure-cone. It has also been noticed that it is less easy to catch starlings roosting at night by dazzling them than it is to catch pigeons. The American robin is also relatively insensitive when dark-adapted.

The increase in sensitivity during dark adaptation is partly due to pupil dilatation, but this can only account for a small part of the increase most of which is dependent on retinal changes. These appear to be of two kinds. Some of the effect is brought about by the regeneration of visual pigment which occurs in the dark. In conditions of vitamin A deficiency it has been shown, in the rat at least, that there is a loss of visual pigment [79, 85, 179] and this loss is accompanied by a gradually decreasing power of dark adaptation leading to a condition of complete night blindness [43, 79, 110]. In man it is well known that night blindness can occur in cases of long-standing malnutrition with vitamin A deficiency. However, the increase in concentration of visual pigment during dark adaptation is not sufficient to account for the millionfold increase in sensitivity shown by a rod-dominated retina. There must be some other mechanism in addition. This other mechanism appears to be a change in the neural organization of the retina which has the effect of decreasing its summatory activity in light adaptation [8]. Such a change has been demonstrated in the cat retina [17] by electrophysiological methods. Here it was found that the inhibitory effect of stimulating areas adjacent to a receptive field (Chapter 2) is only present if the retina is light-adapted; if the retina is dark-adapted, stimulation always has an excitatory effect. This was true for the rods as well as for the cones. In the pure-rod, but by no means typical, retina of *Hemidactylus* it has been found that dark adaptation takes place in two stages [72] as it does in a mixed retina. Since only one type of visual cell is present this break in the course of dark adaptation must be due to some change in the neural organization of the retina. There is also some evidence that, in the mixed retina of man, cone activity in the early stages of dark adaptation can inhibit the rod discharges [83]

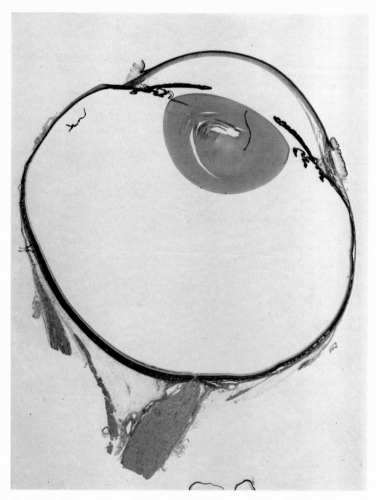

PLATE 9. A diurnal eye. Section through the eye of the California ground squirrel, *Citellus beecheyi*, showing the large posterior chamber and somewhat flattened lens ($\times$ 9·8).

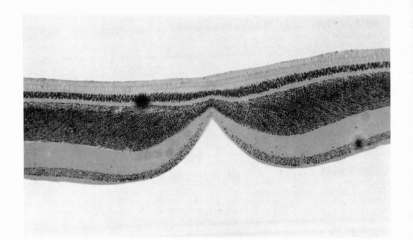

PLATE 10a. The bird fovea. Section through the starling retina showing the deep pit of the central fovea. The nuclear layers are thinner at the fovea, the cells being displaced to the sides causing a thickening of the surrounding layers (× 120).

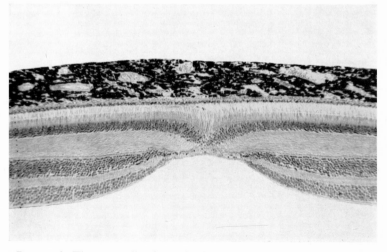

PLATE 10b. The mammalian fovea. Section through the retina of the rhesus monkey showing the shallow central fovea (× 98).

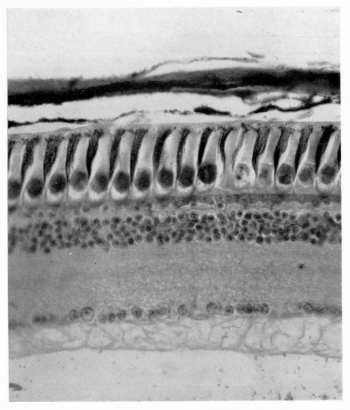

PLATE 11. The gecko retina. Section through the retina of a nocturnal gecko, *Hemidactylus turcicus*, showing the very nearly equal numbers of visual cells and ganglion cells ($\times$ 380).

PLATE 12. The tapetum. Section through the outer retina and back of the eye of a cat showing the tapetum, a very regular structure lying just outside the visual cells ($\times$ 630).

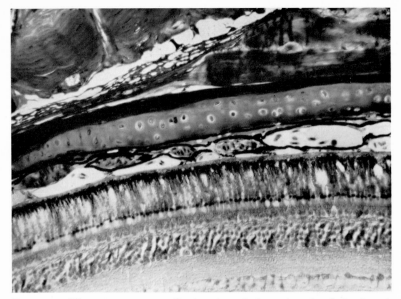

PLATE 13a. Pigment movements. Section through the retina of a dark-adapted frog. The epithelial pigment is retracted leaving the visual cells uncovered (× 253).

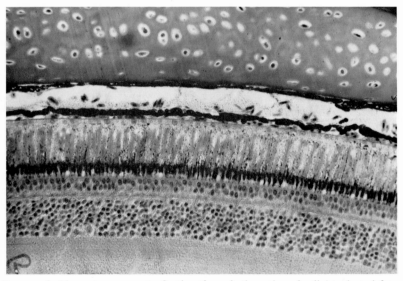

PLATE 13b. Pigment movements. Section through the retina of a light-adapted frog. The epithelial pigment has advanced nearly as far as the external limiting membrane forming a shield to protect the sensitive rods from incoming light (× 253).

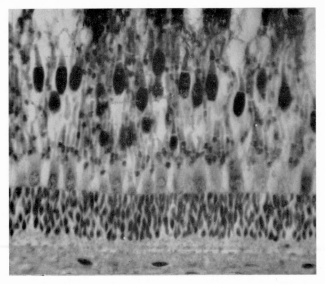

PLATE 14a. Visual cell movements. Section through the visual cell layer of a teleost fish, the bleak, during dark adaptation. The cones have moved away from the external limiting membrane towards the pigment epithelium (× 490).

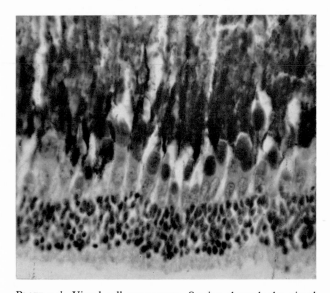

PLATE 14b. Visual cell movements. Section through the visual cell layer of the bleak during light adaptation. The cones have moved back on to the external limiting membrane and the epithelial pigment has advanced towards it (× 490).

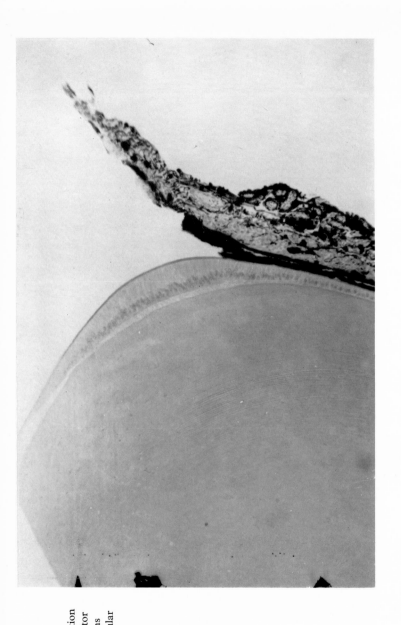

PLATE 15. The annular pad. Section through the equator of the tortoise lens showing the annular pad partially in contact with the ciliary processes (× 133).

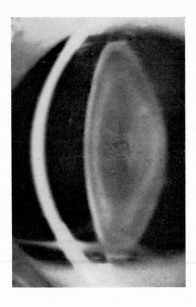

PLATE 16a. Mammalian accommodation. Photograph of the human lens changes on accommodation. Left, unaccommodated

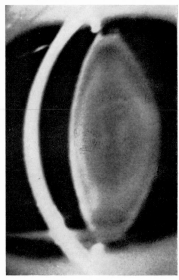

PLATE 16b. Mammalian accommodation. Right, accommodated. Note the increase in curvature of the lens on accommodation.

6. Vision Round the Clock

It would be quite wrong to suggest that the vertebrates are divided into only two groups, those which are diurnal in habit and those which are nocturnal in habit. Many species show activity both by night and by day and these are often especially active in the twilight hours around sunset and sunrise. Animals capable of twenty-four-hour activity are to be found among the teleost fish, which are seldom either strictly diurnal or strictly nocturnal, the frogs, the slit-pupilled reptiles and the larger terrestrial mammals. All these depend on vision, although smell and hearing may also be important, and all, therefore, have eyes which are adapted, in one way or another, to allow visual activity under a wide range of illuminations.

The large terrestrial mammals, ungulates, elephants and large carnivores, such as wolves, bears and lions, have no special retinal or pupillary adaptations such as are found in frogs, teleost fish, reptiles and birds. These animals all have mixed rod and cone retinae. They have large eyes giving an extensive retinal area and a large retinal image, but the visual cells are no bigger than those of small animals. Their rods give them a good sensitivity at low illuminations, while they have enough cones to provide a reasonable visual acuity within the large retinal image. The rather dim retinal image is compensated for by a tapetum which, in effect, increases its brightness by making it possible to use the incoming light twice over. Vision is not equally important to all these species. The elephant, with its relatively small eyes, can be approached quite close from in front so long as the hunter makes a minimum of noise and so long as the wind is in the right direction, while it is important to keep out of sight of a giraffe. The giraffe eye is, perhaps, the biggest among the vertebrates although the horse eye runs it very close. The visual acuity of the elephant is not nearly so good as that of the horse. For an elephant to recognize two points as separate they must subtend an angle of 10

57

minutes 20 seconds at its eye [3]. The angle for the horse is 3 minutes 15 seconds [97] while for the chimpanzee with its well-developed fovea it is only 26 seconds [177]. For comparison the relevant angle for the strictly nocturnal rat is 20 minutes [105]. These eyes usually have a central area where the density of cones is greater and the number of bipolar and ganglion cells is increased. This arrangement reaches its final form in the primates and man where a predominantly rod retina, useful for night vision, surrounds a pure-cone fovea with a high visual acuity but a very low sensitivity. The human fovea is virtually night blind while the acuity of the peripheral retina is extremely poor.

Frogs, teleost fish and birds have special retinal mechanisms to allow efficient retinal activity at a wide variety of illumination levels. In these species the processes of the pigment epithelial cells extend between the visual cells right down to the external limiting membrane and within these processes there is an extensive movement of pigment in response to changes in the ambient illumination. In the dark-adapted eye the pigment is retracted so that it lies just inside the pigment epithelium leaving the visual cells uncovered and exposed to light entering the eye (Plate 13a). In light adaptation the pigment migrates inwards until it lies almost against the external limiting membrane (Plate 13b) thus shielding the sensitive rod outer segments from the incoming light. The visual cells themselves often move as well. In the dark-adapted state the rod myoids contract bringing the cells nearer to the external limiting membrane and clear of the retracted epithelial pigment. At the same time the cone myoids elongate so that the cones move outwards towards the pigment epithelium (Plate 14a). In light adaptation the reverse changes occur. The rod myoids elongate carrying the rods out towards the pigment epithelium and beyond the protective screen of expanded epithelial pigment, while the cone myoids contract pulling these cells back near to the external limiting membrane and in front of the pigment screen (Plate 14b). Thus the cones are exposed to the light while the rods are protected from it. Even in the light-adapted eye the cone outer segments tend to be buried in pigment. This arrangement provides an optical isolation of individual cone outer segments and so probably helps visual acuity. In the pure-cone retinae of such different species as the squirrels and the lizards the cone outer segments are always buried in epithelial pigment although these retinae show no motor adaptations to illumination changes. The only retinae in which rod outer segments are enveloped in pigment are those of the nocturnal geckos (Plate 11). This seems to be an expression of their derivation from diurnal pure-cone ancestors and probably also helps to account for the rather good visual acuity of these species.

These changes in the position of the epithelial pigment and the visual cells in response to light and dark are collectively known as the retinal photomechanical changes. A great deal of work has been done in an effort to determine the mechanisms behind these reactions; are they under nervous control or are they, perhaps, a response to hormonal changes produced by light? On the whole the results have been very disappointing and no firm conclusions have been reached. That the photomechanical changes are not entirely under nervous control is obvious from the fact that they take place in the excised eye [2], but, on the other hand, they are affected by nerve poisons such as strychnine and naphthalene and these effects are much reduced if the optic nerve is cut [40]. The changes are surprisingly slow, taking from a half to one hour to complete. Perhaps this is because the natural changes of illumination at sunrise and sunset are relatively slow too, but the similar changes in pigment position to be observed in the cephalopod eye are very much faster, being complete in a few minutes [226]. Vertebrate photomechanical changes are also affected by temperature [66], oxygen tension (in fish), time of day [132, 220] and emotional disturbance [65]. These factors are a serious complication in experiments designed to study the control of retinal movements. No experiments have yet been performed in which all the conditions were adequately controlled and this is probably the reason why the results of such experiments have been so confused and disappointing. The whole subject needs to be re-examined by means of better controlled experiments. Not only do we not know whether the photomechanical reactions are under nervous control, we also do not know whether the shortening of the visual cell myoids represents an active contraction, nor have we any idea of the mechanism of the myoid lengthenings and shortenings. The pigment movements are known to be due to the movements of pigment granules within the epithelial cell processes, which do not themselves change in position, but we have no idea how light and darkness produce these movements. There are some odd anomalies. In the frog, one type of rod exhibits movements while another type remains stationary. In species with double cones (but not in pure-cone retinae which show no photomechanical changes) the principal member moves in response to light and darkness while the accessory member remains still. But there is no obvious morphological difference between the two myoids.

There are, therefore, two methods in the vertebrates whereby the amount of light reaching the retinal visual cells can be regulated. There are the photomechanical changes and the changes in pupil size and where one method is well developed the other is usually poorly developed and may be altogether absent. Photomechanical changes are most active in teleost fish where the pupil is often quite immobile, while mammals have very reactive pupils and no photomechanical changes at all [64]. Pupil changes, where they occur, are usually much faster than the photomechanical reactions and may, therefore, be more useful. Strictly nocturnal species which never ordinarily emerge in daylight, or strictly diurnal species which stop their activity between sunset and sunrise may show neither photomechanical changes nor pupil movements. This is true of the small nocturnal rodents and also of the diurnal lampreys, turtles, lizards and snakes. Nocturnal reptiles have very active pupils which close completely to a vertical slit but very slight, if any, photomechanical changes. Birds have extremely active pupils but it is doubtful whether they react satisfactorily to light; the photomechanical changes are fairly rapid and quite extensive.

Where the pupil is mobile contraction in the light is always a more rapid process than dilatation in the dark. This probably reflects the fact that light adaptation is much quicker than dark adaptation, as well as the importance of quickly shielding a sensitive retina from unduly bright lights. Contraction is brought about by the circular sphincter muscle of the iris. All mobile pupils have an iris sphincter but not all have a radial dilatator muscle. In some small mammals, whose pupils are not very active, what dilatation is possible is due to the natural elasticity of the iris stroma, and the dilatator is lacking. Teleost fish with their immobile pupils have no iris muscles at all. Some elasmobranch fish have very sluggish pupillary responses to light and in these the movements are not under nervous control but are due to a direct effect of light on the iris tissue. In the amphibia the pupil is regulated nervously and in some species there is also a direct light effect. This is the case in frogs but not in the South African clawed toad, *Xenopus*, whose isolated iris does not contract on illumination [217]. A similar direct light effect has also been claimed in the dog after prolonged dark adaptation [96]. Where the pupil is under nervous control, as it is in all species above the fishes, contraction is due to a reflex triggered off by light falling on the retina. In all animals except mammals the pupils are independent of one another and one can contract while the other remains stationary or dilates according to circumstances. In mammals there is a consensual reflex; light shining on one eye produces contraction in the pupil of the other. A consensual reflex has been claimed in pigeons but here the contraction of the pupil of the unilluminated eye appears to be due to stimulation by light penetrating from behind through the other eye and the head. Birds' eyes almost meet within the head and the backs of the two are very close together. In owls, which have frontal eyes so that one cannot be stimulated by light falling on the other, there is no apparent consensual reflex [128].

Of the two methods for regulating the amount of light reaching the visual cells, the photomechanical changes are phylogenetically older; they reach their highest development in the teleost fish. As one ascends the evolutionary scale the pupil gradually takes over until, in the mammals, it has the sole responsibility. In birds, both mechanisms appear to be highly developed. The pupils are extremely active and the photomechanical changes are extensive. There is, however, some doubt as to how important the illumination level is in determining the size of the avian pupil. Birds are the most eye-minded of all vertebrates with the highest visual acuity (the visual acuity of the hawk is said to be eight times that of man and although this figure has been questioned [169] it is certainly very high) and it must be very important to them to cut spherical aberration to an absolute minimum. It may be that the active pupil contraction (and the pupils of diurnal birds tend to be small) is mainly to stop down the lens and that the regulation of light is largely in the hands of the retinal visual cell and pigment movements.

We have seen that the vertebrates can be roughly divided into three categories according to their habits with regard to the external illumination level. There are the diurnal vertebrates which have relatively insensitive eyes developed for a high visual acuity and incapable of vision at low illuminations. These eyes tend to be on the large side, to have shallow anterior chambers and deep posterior chambers and to have a retina whose visual cells are predominantly or all cones. Diurnal animals always have some type of ocular colour filter, always yellow but sometimes red and orange as well. These colour filters range from the yellow cornea of really diurnal fishes through the yellow lenses of lampreys, the diurnal geckos, snakes and squirrels to the coloured oil droplets in the cones of frogs, diurnal lizards and birds. In addition there is the macular pigmentation of man and the primates. The nocturnal veterbrates may have large eyes if they are visually minded (bush baby, owls) or small ones if vision is relatively unimportant (rats, mice). The anterior chamber is deep with a large cornea and pupil and a powerful lens which may even be spherical. The retina is either pure-rod or dominated by rods; it also shows much convergence of visual cells on to optic nerve fibres and is, therefore, very sensitive but with a poor visual acuity. The lens and cornea are always colourless and where there are oil droplets in the visual cells these are also colourless. There may be a tapetum. Nocturnal animals, mostly reptiles but also the small cats and some fish and amphibia, which like to emerge in the daylight and perhaps bask in the sun, have extremely active pupils which close, often completely, to a vertical slit. Such a pupil provides excellent protection for a sensitive nocturnal retina. Vertebrates which are capable of activity at all illumination levels have eyes in which the proportions of the anterior and posterior chambers are more nearly balanced (Figure 13). The eyes may well be big. The retina always contains both rods and cones, the proportions of these varying with the illu-

FIG. 13. Twenty-four-hour eyes. The general structure of the eye in three species which have both day and night vision. [208].

mination preferences of the owner. There is usually a specially developed central area in the retina, where the proportion of cones is high, surrounded by a peripheral area with many rods. In man and the primates the central area contains a pure-cone fovea. There tends to be some mechanism, photomechanical changes or a mobile pupil, for protecting the sensitive rods from being over-exposed to light in the daytime. There is often a tapetum. There are, of course, all gradations between these three groups. Apart from the nocturnal species with slit pupils there are others which, although night hunters, apparently have good vision during the day. The eagle owl, *Bubo bubo*, which has been shown to be able to find food by sight in a light too dim to reveal anything to a human observer, can recognize, in full sunlight, diurnal predators invisible to the human eye [169]. The little owl, too, can hunt quite successfully in the light although it prefers darkness. Other owls (e.g. the tawny owl) seldom appear during the day. Perhaps the eagle owls should be classed as twenty-four-hour animals in spite of their preference for night hunting; they are among the biggest of the owls and have enormous eyes. All owls have a good number of cones although rods predominate in their retinae. The Manx shearwater is another bird active by both night and day and it is known to possess more rods and to show more convergence in its retina than more strictly diurnal birds [131]. Swifts and swallows also hunt small insects on the wing far into the dusk and must have excellent dim-light vision as well as being perfectly at home in full daylight. Other animals (e.g. rabbits) are mainly active during the morning and evening twilight periods and have no special adaptations for vision at the extremes of high or low illumination.

7. Accommodation

In all terrestrial vertebrates the cornea is the main refractive surface of the eye and the lens often acts as a fine adjustment, its shape or position being altered to change the final position of the retinal image. These lens alterations are known as accommodation.

In man the normal eye at rest is set to focus images of objects at about twenty feet on to the retinal visual cells and such an eye is said to be emmetropic. If the object to be observed is nearer to the eye, the image will be thrown behind the visual cell layer and in order to bring it back into the right position the lens will have to become more convex – accommodation has to be exercised. Sometimes the eyeball is too short and in these cases the image will once again be focused behind the visual cell layer even when the eye is at rest. Such an eye is called hypermetropic or long-sighted and it has to exercise accommodation to bring images of any but the most distant objects on to the visual cell outer segments. Convex spectacles for near work are prescribed in these cases. These increase the total power of the eye's optical system and so bring the image forwards. In other cases the eyeball is too long and images of distant objects are then focused in front of the visual cells. These eyes are myopic or short-sighted. Accommodation will only make matters worse and such eyes have to be corrected with concave spectacles which diverge the light rays and throw the image farther back. There is no magic about the figure of twenty feet, it just happens to be a convenient distance for the human eye at rest. The normal eyes of many animals are hypermetropic if their objects of interest tend to be at greater distances, while others which, owing to their particular habitat or for other reasons, have no occasion for or possibility of examining distant objects may be normally myopic. Not all animals are capable of exercising accommodation. Some have eyes which make it unnecessary – the lens may have a large depth of focus or the visual cells may be unusually long –

while others, especially the small mammals, have such poor vision anyway that fine adjustments are simply not worth while.

In opthalmology the power of a lens is expressed in dioptres. The dioptric power is the reciprocal of the focal length in metres. Degrees of myopia and hypermetropia are usually expressed in terms of the number of dioptres of the lens necessary to give normal vision; thus a myopic eye which needs a concave lens of four dioptres would be said to have four dioptres of myopia. Accommodation can be described in the same manner. For instance, a normal human eye is focused for distant objects when it is at rest and in order to see an object clearly at 0·2 metres it will have to increase the power of its lens system until it can focus on an object at this distance. This is called exercising 5 dioptres of accommodation. A hypermetrope who ordinarily has to accommodate by, say, 1·5 dioptres in order to see clearly at a distance must increase his accommodation by the same 5 dioptres to see clearly at 0·2 metres. Therefore he has to accommodate by a total of 6·5 dioptres in order to focus an object at this distance. The normal young adult human eye is capable of exercising about 10 dioptres of accommodation, but this power is gradually lost during the succeeding years until at sixty-five the eye is virtually incapable of accommodation and, except for the more myopic, reading glasses are a necessity.

The site of visual excitation in the eye is the outer segments of the visual cells and this is where the image of an external object must be focused if there is to be clear vision. The outer segments may be very long especially in nocturnal animals. This is primarily a device for increasing sensitivity for it increases the amount of visual pigment present and so the chances of the capture of light quanta. However, long outer segments should decrease the need for accommodation by increasing the range of useful positions of the focused image. There is a limit to the possible length of the visual-cell outer segments since the longer these are the more separated are the inner segments and nuclei of the cells from their source of nutrition in the choroid. It is not certain how far this device of lengthening the outer segment really affects accommodation, especially as it is characteristic of nocturnal animals many of which appear to have little need of especially well-focused images. In any case the small eyes and large, nearly spherical lenses of many nocturnal animals will provide a greater depth of focus than is present in larger eyes so that any accommodation mechanism is much less necessary. Another situation, which has been thought to have the same effect as lengthening the visual-cell outer segments, is found in the fruit bats [208]. Here the choroid forms a series of projecting papillae and the retina is thrown into radial folds to fit in with them. This results in some visual cells being farther from and some nearer to the lens. The fruit bats are strictly nocturnal and have a pure-rod retina; they have no accommodatory mechanism which could affect the lens. However, it has been calculated that the odd arrangement of this retina would only give the equivalent of 1·5 dioptres of accommodation and this seems hardly enough to be worth while [152]. It is more likely that the special arrangement of choroid and retina in these species is a device for increasing the retinal nutrition since capillaries penetrate the retina from the choroid at the tip of each choroidal papilla.

Some eyes are not symmetrical about the lens; the axial length of the eyeball changes continuously in the vertical meridian. This produces what is known as a 'ramp' retina, different areas of which will be at different distances from the lens. In this type of eye, which is present in the horse and, to a much more exaggerated extent, in the rays, distant objects will be focused on the inferior part of the retina which is nearer to the lens and nearer objects on the superior part with a smooth transition between them. The horse has no means of changing the focal length of its lens but can change the position of the image within the retina by tilting its head. An eye with a ramp retina is set to a distant focus for objects overhead and to a near one for objects underneath.

A pupil which contracts to give a pinhole aperture will also reduce the need for accommodation. Such an aperture produces a pretty sharp image regardless of the distances of the retina and the external object. Such pupils are only found in nocturnal animals and are primarily useful in protecting a sensitive retina from bright lights. They are present in some dogfish, in the rays, the nocturnal geckos, some ungulates especially camels, the domestic cat and the palm civet.

The actual mechanism of accommodation differs between the different orders of vertebrates. Some, as in man, provide accommodation for near vision, the resting eye being focused for distance; others (lampreys, teleost fish) provide accommodation for distant vision. In some cases the shape of the lens is altered, in others its position. Alteration of the shape of the lens may be brought about by actually squeezing it or it may be by releasing a normal tension and allowing its own elasticity to take effect.

Accommodation in the vertebrate eye is almost always achieved by means of muscles situated inside the eyeball – the intra-ocular muscles – but in the lampreys the relevant muscle is outside the eye. There is a massive muscle, known as the cornealis muscle, lying to one side of the eyeball with its tendon inserted into the primary spectacle, a transparent window in the skin of the head covering the cornea. Contraction of the cornealis muscle pulls on the spectacle thus exerting a backward pressure on the cornea and also on the lens which is in direct contact with it. This pressure pushes the lens back farther into the eye so that it approaches the retina throwing the retinal image farther back and thus making the eye more hypermetropic. At rest the lamprey eye is myopic by human standards and the effect of accommodation is to improve more distant vision.

In the elasmobranchs accommodation is also brought about by moving the lens, but in this case the muscle concerned is intra-ocular and the lens is moved forward away from the retina when the muscle contracts. This provides accommodation for near vision which is very necessary as the elasmobranch eye is several dioptres hypermetropic.

Teleost fish have an intra-ocular muscle, the *retractor lentis* or campanular muscle, whose tendon is actually inserted into the lens. Contraction of this muscle certainly moves the lens sideways and is also thought to move it backwards nearer the retina; the teleost eye is usually believed to be myopic [208] so that accommodation would be for distant vision, as in the lamprey. However, more recent work on the living eyes of salmon and two other teleost species, both American (the alewife, *Alosa pseudoharengus*, and the silversides, *Menidia menidia*,) suggest that this is certainly not always true. In the salmon the lens has so great a depth of focus that accommodation would appear to be unnecessary and the images of distant objects have been shown to fall within the retina so that the eye is not myopic. Further, in this species contraction of the campanula muscle simply moves the lens laterally and does not alter its distance from the retina. Examination of the eyes of the alewife and silversides have also shown that, so far from being myopic, they are actually hypermetropic in water [19]; these fish appear to have considerable powers of accommodation, up to 18 dioptres in the case of the alewife. These exceptions throw some doubt on the generalization that the teleost eye is myopic and accommodates for distant vision through movement of the lens towards the retina owing to contraction of the campanula muscle, but work is required on many more species before there can be any certainty.

With the amphibia we come to the problem of seeing both in air and under water. Under water the cornea is eliminated as a refractive surface and the whole optical power of the eye rests in the lens which, in fish, is spherical and, therefore, powerful; the fish cornea is usually flat. In amphibia the cornea is much more curved and in terrestrial and amphibious species becomes the main refractive element in the eye. Amphibia exercise accommodation in much the same way as elasmobranch fish. They have a muscle, the *protractor lentis*, one end of which is inserted at the corneo-scleral junction while the other end passes through the root of the iris and is inserted into a rudimentary ciliary body. The lens is attached to this ciliary body by means of delicate zonular fibres and contraction of the *protractor lentis* muscle pulls the ciliary body and, through it, the zonular fibres and lens forwards towards the cornea and away from the retina. Amphibian accommodation is, therefore, for near vision. It is not, however, very extensive having a maximum extent of only about 5 dioptres. Really efficient vision both in air and water is first found in some aquatic birds. Purely aquatic amphibian species like the newts are emmetropic under water and become severely myopic in the air. Amphibious and terrestrial species are emmetropic in air and, of course, become strongly hypermetropic under water. Their power of accommodation will help a little but is never enough fully to compensate for the optical elimination of the cornea consequent

on immersion in water. Many amphibia appear to have no accommodation at all, particularly the most secretive species. Most amphibious species have long outer segments to their visual cells and
this could somewhat reduce the need for accommodation. They also
feed in air and may not need very efficient underwater vision.

In reptiles (except the snakes), birds and mammals accommodation
is no longer accomplished by changing the position of the lens. Its
shape is changed instead and in all cases the lens becomes more convex and accommodation is exerted for near vision. In reptiles and
birds the lens is actually squeezed so that it becomes longer from
back to front and the curvature of its anterior part is increased.
Among the reptiles, lizards, especially, and tortoises, to a lesser extent, have rapid and extensive powers of accommodation. They have
a large and well-developed ciliary body containing a powerful
striated ciliary muscle and prominent ciliary processes. These latter
are tall, fin-like structures which make firm contact with the lens into
which the tips are actually fused. Contraction of the ciliary muscle,
therefore, exerts a direct pressure all round at the lens equator
distorting the lens so that its curvature, and thus its focal power, is
increased. The lens comes, as it were, to meet the ciliary body by developing an annular pad (Plate 15), an equatorial thickening brought
about by an enormous lengthening of the epithelial cells in this
region. The lens itself is soft and so more easily deformed. The
vitreous, on the other hand, is especially viscous thus supporting the
posterior pole of the lens and preventing a bodily backwards movement. Inserted into the sclera in a circle round the base of the cornea
is a series of small bony plates called the scleral ossicles. These
strengthen the sclera in the region of the ciliary body so that the pull
exerted by contraction of the ciliary muscle does not deform the eyeball. The crocodiles and alligators have lost the scleral ossicles and
have a much reduced annular pad to the lens although this is still in
direct contact with the ciliary processes. The ciliary muscle is
rather poorly developed. Accommodation in these large reptiles is
said to be present but slow and slight. It has been suggested that
these, being nocturnal animals, have little need of accommodation
[208]; but the alligator, at least, is thought to be emmetropic in air

which would make it 15 to 20 dioptres hypermetropic under water if accommodation were impossible. The snakes are in a special position. In the course of their evolution from lacertilian ancestors they have lost the scleral ossicles, the annular pad and the ciliary muscles. These losses, as well as certain other features such as the absence of the lacertilian cone oil droplets and the replacement of eyelids by a spectacle, are thought to indicate a degeneration of the eyes during the burrowing period when the snakes also lost their limbs [207]. In the modern snakes the ciliary body is out of contact with the lens and has no musculature. Instead there is a collection of muscle fibres at the root of the iris and these are responsible for accommodation. When they contract they exert pressure on the vitreous which in its turn pushes the lens forward towards the cornea. The intra-ocular pressure is raised and the whole eyeball is somewhat elongated. Both the elongation of the eyeball and the forward displacement of the lens accommodate the eye for near vision. Lizards need good and rapid accommodation, for not only are they extremely agile but they feed on quick-flying insects. Snakes do not need and have not got such excellent powers of accommodation.

The accommodatory mechanism in birds is the same as that in lizards. They have powerful striated ciliary muscles, a special scleral muscle known as Crampton's muscle, a soft lens with a well-developed annular pad and scleral ossicles. Some birds, such as owls and hawks, also have an extra scleral muscle which deforms the cornea increasing its curvature. Birds' powers of accommodation are probably greater than those of any other vertebrates, and this is especially true of certain aquatic birds which apparently can see under water as well as they can see in the air. In some birds the eye is an efficient instrument in the air and virtually useless under water. This appears to be true of such diving birds as the terns which spot their fish from above, dive blind and often miss. Other eyes may be well adapted for underwater vision and poor instruments out of water. Penguins, for instance, can chase fish by sight but are badly myopic in the air. But many birds, cormorants, diving ducks, loons, auks and dippers have truly amphibious vision and these have terrific powers of accommodation so that the great increase in the power of the lens makes up for the loss of the cornea as a refracting surface. In an investigation [186] of the eye of the common dipper (*Cinclus cinclus*) it was compared with those of some other passerine birds, among them the American robin (*Turdus migratorius*). The dipper appears to be just as much at home under water as on land, swimming expertly at the bottom of streams where it collects the larvae of water insects and chases small fish. From its behaviour it apparently has good vision both in air and water and the investigation confirmed that its eye is emmetropic in air. It has a potential accommodation of up to 48 dioptres and this would compensate for the 40 dioptres of hypermetropia which the resting eye would develop under water. Under the conditions of the experiments the American robin showed 7·5 dioptres of accommodation. The ciliary musculature was similar in both birds, but there was an increase in iris musculature in the dipper suggesting that the iris also plays a part in deforming the lens by pressure. The dipper also had the more spherical lens and in this it resembles the cormorant which can exercise 40 to 50 dioptres of accommodation too. The cormorant hunts fish by eye under water. These birds with amphibious vision have very soft lenses indeed, enormously powerful accommodatory muscles and very heavy scleral ossicles. The kingfisher is a bird which does not appear to accommodate under water although it is said to see well under these conditions. This bird has two foveae and it has been suggested that the central fovea is adapted for aerial vision while the lateral fovea mediates aquatic vision [120].

The mammalian accommodatory mechanism is quite different from any that has yet been described. In the mammalian eye at rest the lens is held under tension by the sideways pull of the ciliary body communicated to the lens by means of the zonular fibres. When the ciliary muscle contracts the aperture of the circular ciliary body is decreased and the whole body moves forwards towards the cornea. The total effect is to release the tension on the zonular fibres and so to allow the natural elasticity of the lens capsule to come into play (Figure 14). This moulds the lens so that it becomes more convex and accommodates the eye for near vision (Plate 16). In man the lens becomes progressively harder with increasing age and at about forty

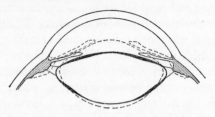

FIG. 14. Mammalian accommodation. Diagram of the anterior part of the human eye and the changes due to accommodation. Full lines indicate the unaccommodated eye, the dotted lines the changes consequent on contraction of the ciliary muscle.

the capsule is less able to affect its shape and accommodation becomes increasingly more difficult until in the succeeding years it is completely lost. This is when the normal eye requires convex reading glasses for near work. If the eye was hypermetropic to begin with reading glasses will be necessary at an earlier age; if it was sufficiently myopic they may never be needed. Many small mammals, especially nocturnal ones, have no accommodation. They mostly have small eyes with large nearly spherical lenses with a considerable depth of focus. Mammals with no accommodation include the rat, mouse, rabbit, hamster and guinea-pig. Cattle and sheep are said to have little or no accommodation, although this is not accepted by all authorities [223]. The cat, dog and rhesus monkey have been shown to have a reasonable amount of accommodation. These animals show a rather different microscopic structure of the ciliary muscle [223] which is, in any case, not striated in mammals. The bush baby has an enormous ciliary muscle and would appear, therefore, to have considerable powers of accommodation. These have never been measured but the bush baby does appear to have good vision in spite of its highly nocturnal eyes. Most wild mammals are slightly (about one dioptre) hypermetropic, 1–2 dioptres in the cat and will only need one dioptre of accommodation to become emmetropic. A second dioptre of accommodation will bring the focus into one metre, which should be sufficient for an animal that does not do close work. Mandrills and baboons are said to be somewhat myopic. Two aquatic mammals, the

European beaver and the otter, have very well-developed ciliary bodies and apparently considerable powers of accommodation since they have good vision both in air and water. In addition, the otter has an enormous sphincter muscle in the iris which squeezes the anterior part of the lens when it contracts. The actual range of otter accommodation has never been measured but this animal is emmetropic or slightly hypermetropic in air and certainly fishes by eye under water; its accommodatory power must be comparable with that of the cormorant or dipper.

8. Binocular Vision and the Judgement of Depth and Distance

Except for the bats and some at least of the dolphins, which do it mostly by ear, animals can only make accurate distance judgements by eye. Smell can be used for the perception of distant objects but it is an inaccurate way of estimating the actual position of an object in space. There are many visual clues which may be used in assessing distance. If the real size of an object is known its distance can be judged by its apparent size, the smaller it appears the farther off it must be. Objects which partially obscure others must be the nearer, while those that look dim as well as small are very far away. Then there is perspective, as every artist knows, and parallax. If an object appears to move in the contrary direction when the head is moved it must be in front of one which moves in the same direction and the difference in the amount of apparent movement gives a good indication of the relative distances of two objects in the visual field. All these clues can be, and constantly are, used by one-eyed individuals [202] and by those animals with lateral eyes which have little or no binocular vision. Birds and snakes can often be seen to make rapid 'peering' movements of the head before pecking or striking at their food. They are using parallax to determine its precise position.

However, in man at least, the most accurate method of judging distance and solidity is by means of stereoscopic vision. This appears to depend on the simultaneous appreciation of the slightly, but not too widely, dissimilar images from corresponding points of the two retinae. The human foveae are corresponding points. Stereoscopic vision is extremely accurate. Under experimental conditions in which all monocular clues to relative distance, such as overlapping or shadows, are absent it is possible to tell which of three objects is beyond or in front of the others when the displacement is very small indeed. A displacement of only 0·5 mm can be detected at a distance of 340 mm [103]. Stereoscopic vision does not function at more than fifty to eighty feet.

For stereoscopic vision to be possible it is obviously essential to have binocular vision; that is the faculty of viewing an object with both eyes simultaneously and seeing one and not two images. In the past it has been suggested that only the mammals enjoy binocular vision because only the mammals have an incomplete decussation of the optic nerves at the chiasma and so a representation of images from both eyes on one side in the brain. This seems to be most unlikely. It is not really credible that a hawk, for instance, with its frontal eyes giving a large binocular visual field and its well-known accuracy when stooping, should see not one small bird or rodent but two. It is probable that all animals with binocular fields which include a high acuity area such as is given by a fovea, not only have binocular vision but also have stereoscopic vision. In this connexion it is interesting that experiments on one of the gannets, which has lateral eyes and only one central fovea in each eye so that it cannot use them for binocular vision, have shown that its judgement of distance is apparently not very good. If fish are fastened on to floating bits of wood the gannet, diving on to the bait, does not know when to check its flight and may even transfix the wood with its beak. Under natural conditions this lack of distance perception does not matter so much since the gannet normally dives into yielding water. Hawks have two foveae in each eye, one central and one lateral, the two latter giving a binocular field with a high visual acuity. Poor distance perception would be fatal to a hawk whose prey is, as often as not, on the hard ground. Vultures have no second fovea in spite of their close relationship to the hawks and eagles. They certainly locate their food by sight for they cannot find carrion if it is covered up in spite of its smell, and they can be deceived by the painted representation of a dead animal. But vultures do not stoop swiftly on their food; they circle round in a leisurely fashion and come down to the ground gradually.

One way of determining whether an animal has depth perception or not is by training it to go to one of two objects of different sizes. If, for instance, an animal has been trained to respond to the larger of two circles and this larger one is then moved so far away that its retinal image is actually the smaller the animal in question will often still respond to the correct circle. In this case it is clearly not reacting to the actual size of the retinal image but must recognize the circle as being larger but farther away. Using this method it has been shown that the carp [106], the stickleback [137], the hen [87] and the blue jay [107] all have respectable depth perception. In the case of the carp depth perception was dependent on binocular vision; the fish could not respond correctly when one eye was removed. The effect of restriction to monocular vision was not tested in the two birds or the stickleback.

Of course binocular vision is only possible where there is some overlapping of the visual fields of the two eyes and, therefore, the more frontally the eyes are placed in the head the greater the part of the visual field which is potentially binocular. Most animals have some binocular field although in those with lateral eyes it may be relatively small. Even the rabbit has a frontal binocular field of approximately 20 degrees. Most animals appear to use binocular vision from choice when circumstances allow it. The horse, whose laterally placed eyes prevent its seeing near objects binocularly, tends to face an approaching object until it comes too near for binocular observation when the animal turns its head and uses monocular vision instead.

The degree to which binocular vision is accompanied by accurate stereoscopic vision is probably determined by the visual acuity within the binocular field. If the eyes are frontally placed in the head the wide binocular field will include the central special area of the retina and a central fovea if there is one. This is true for the domestic cat which has a central special area in its retina and, of course, for hawks and eagles which have lateral foveae as well. Owls have no central fovea but their lateral foveae are so placed as to give a high-acuity binocular field. In some hunting animals which have lateral eyes the fovea may be placed in an extreme temporal position so that the restricted binocular field does include foveal vision. Lizards and some teleost fish, which need good binocular vision but which have lateral eyes, have a single fovea in the far temporal periphery of the retina. Birds which hunt on the wing, such as swallows, have more frontal eyes and, like the hawks, a second temporal fovea as well as a central one which can only serve monocular vision.

To some extent the degree of frontality of the eyes depends on the feeding habits of the owner. There is a tendency for hunting animals to have frontal eyes and large binocular fields, while those which are hunted usually have lateral eyes giving total visual fields which are very large indeed but relatively restricted binocular fields. There are many exceptions, as we have just seen; lizards, hunting fish and many hunting birds have lateral eyes (but acute vision within their small binocular fields), while the hunters *par excellence*, the carnivores, especially those of the cat family, and the hawks, eagles and owls are conspicuous for the extreme frontality of their eyes. These predatory animals are not usually in danger themselves and can, therefore, dispense with a knowledge of what is happening behind them but they need good stereoscopic vision to enable them to pounce or stoop accurately upon their prey. Hunted animals, on the other hand, need to be able to spot danger coming from any direction. The rabbit can see all round its head and even has a posterior binocular field of about 9 degrees. The cat has a binocular field of 130 degrees and a total visual field of 287 degrees. The rabbit, on the other hand, has a frontal binocular field of only 20 degrees but a total visual field of 360 degrees. Hawks have a binocular field of about 50 degrees and owls have 60 degrees to 70 degrees while granivorous birds never have more than 25 degrees and sometimes less than 10 degrees. The homing pigeon, with a binocular field of 24 degrees, has a total visual field of 340 degrees. The binocular field in man is 140 degrees and the total field 180 degrees. The much larger total field of the cat, also with frontal eyes, is due to the large, prominent and highly curved cornea which this animal possesses. The binocular fields of hawks and owls are small compared with those of other frontally-eyed animals because of their tubular eyes and relatively small retinal areas which restrict their monocular fields.

A few animals have no binocular field at all, the lampreys, the hammerhead sharks, a few large-headed teleosts, some amphibians, one genus of penguin (*Spheniscus*) and the larger whales. Those penguins, without binocular fields, can be observed to weave and sway a good deal while examining an object. It is not know whether such birds as the toucans and hornbills have any binocular field around their enormous bills. In some animals, such as the chameleons and some fish, there is no binocular field when the eyes are at rest, but one can be produced by convergence. Those animals which have any eye movements at all can, and do, converge in order to enlarge the anterior binocular field.

The bitterns, when alarmed, freeze among the rushes with the bill pointing straight up into the air thus providing themselves with a useful camouflage. If the binocular field were to remain along the direction of the bill the bird in this position would be looking uselessly at the sky. Actually the bittern is able to turn its eyes so far ventrally that it has binocular vision under its own bill and can see truly forward parallel to the ground. The snipes, on the other hand, have their eyes set so far back in the head that their posterior binocular field is probably larger than their anterior one. In feeding, the snipes thrust their long bills so far into the ground after worms and other prey that they would be extremely vulnerable if they did not have good vision behind the head.

Some animals which are certainly not predatory have conspicuously frontal eyes. This is true of the primates which, except for the bush babies and other nocturnal species, also have central foveae. The primates use their hands for fine manipulations and for this they use binocular, and apparently stereoscopic vision. Another non-predatory group of animals with frontal eyes contains some of the deep-sea fish. These live at depths where the level of illumination is very low indeed. A little daylight may penetrate but most of the illumination is from luminous organisms and the light organs of the fish themselves. Their binocular vision appears to be an adaptation to these low illumination levels. In human vision the lowest illumination visible to the dark-adapted eye is less by about ten per cent for binocular than for monocular vision, and although this is of little interest to man with the wide range of intensities available to him, it may be of great importance to these fish which live under conditions where light is at a premium [216]. Similar living conditions in light of low intensity may make the frontal eyes of the nocturnal primates useful too. Bush babies have no fovea or special area in their retinae and, therefore, seem unlikely to have acute stereoscopic vision. Their eyes are very large and highly sensitive, with many retinal rods and a tapetum unusually efficient as a reflecting surface. Their large binocular visual fields probably also assist their vision at low illuminations.

9. The Perception of Movement

One of the most vital and fundamental functions of the eye is the perception of movement. This capacity is absolutely necessary for any animal that moves and especially if its prey and predators are also mobile. The faster an animal normally moves or the faster its prey moves the more acute must its perception of movement be. Now the stimulus value of a moving object depends not only on the actual capacity of the eye to perceive and evaluate movement but also on the general importance of moving objects to the animal in question. Hunted animals may react more strongly to moving objects seen vaguely by the peripheral retina because any such object may well be a predator and, therefore, dangerous to them. In addition, the amount of competition provided by other visual sensations is a factor. For this reason, moving objects perceived by the generally inferior retinal periphery may have great attention value just because peripheral vision is usually poor. The physiological equipment for movement perception in the peripheral retina is, as a rule, much less good than that of the central retina but moving objects seen out of the corner of the eye are nearly always attended to.

Species which feed on live animals will usually only take prey if it is moving. Frogs and toads can starve to death while surrounded by dead flies which are, of course, motionless. Experiments on toads have shown that the movements of their food need not be natural ones. They will take insects or even bits of meat which are mounted on a moving platform. They are even able to appreciate apparent motion and will eat food which is itself stationary if the environment is made to move instead [119]. Perch also will only snap at moving bait, but here the response depends on the direction rather than the speed or amount of movement. They do not respond if the movement is too rapid [35]. Hedgehogs were found to reject the small invertebrates, which are their natural food, if the animals were dead or moribund or immobile for any other reason [67]. However, hedge-hogs will take non-natural food such as meat or fish when it is stationary. It is noticeable that cats, for instance, are apparently unable to see a stationary ball, or at least they take no interest in it, but will immediately chase it if it is rolled along the ground. And it is probable that hawks and eagles cannot see distant small animals unless they move. This lack of interest in or inability to recognize stationary prey by predators is apparently the reason why so many hunted animals 'freeze' when in danger.

The speed of a moving object is important. If it moves too slowly its actual movement is not perceived, as when one regards the hands of a clock. One knows that the hands must be moving because in time they change position but the movement itself is invisible. On the other hand if an object moves too fast, as for instance a bullet, its image may not rest in one position on the retina for long enough to cause a visual sensation.

One important factor in the perception of movement is the fineness of the retinal 'grain' (see Chapter 2). Images moving within the receptive field of a single optic nerve fibre are not usually seen to be moving, the image must impinge on a second receptive field before its change of position can be recognized. Therefore the smaller the receptive field the less the amount of movement that can be ap-preciated. This means that the perception of movement is usually more acute in a cone retina than it is in a rod retina for the receptive fields of the former tend to be smaller. For the same reason move-ment is more accurately perceived by us with the fovea than with the peripheral retina although it has more attention value in the peri-phery. Altogether the higher the visual acuity the more acute the per-ception of movement.

There are however, certain ganglion cells in some retinae, which show a more specific response to movement. With microelectrode recording it has been shown that about one third of the ganglion cells in the rabbit retina produced an electrical response to movement across the receptive field and that for a given ganglion cell this re-sponse was to movement in one direction only [18]. Similar movement detectors have been described in the retinae of frogs [136] and pigeons [135] and in the higher centres of several laboratory animals, in the optic nerve [126] and tectum of the frog [127] in the lateral geniculate nucleus of the rabbit [4] and the visual cortex of the cat [114].

Another important factor in the perception of movement is the phenomenon of the persistence of vision. The appreciation of a transient retinal stimulus does not cease immediately the stimulus is removed. Instead it persists for a short interval, the length of which depends on the state of adaptation of the eye and the intensity of the stimulus. If a stimulating image is moving across the retina it will, in consequence, leave a sort of trail behind it. If a black and white sectored disc is observed rotating the individual sectors can be recognized if the rotation is sufficiently slow, but as it goes faster the disc will appear to flicker as the persisting image of one sector begins to merge with that of the next. If the rotation is fast enough all perception of movement is lost and the disc appears to be of a steady uniform grey. The speed of rotation at which the flickering appearance is just lost is known as the flicker-fusion frequency and this speed gives a good idea of the ability of the eye to follow movement under the given conditions of the experiment. Much work has been done on the flicker-fusion frequency both in man and animals. It has been found that the fusion frequency is higher for the cones than for the rods which is not surprising since cone reactions are always faster than rod reactions. Linked to this is the fact that the fusion frequency is higher in light adaptation than in dark adaptation. It is also dependent on the brightness of the retinal image; the brighter the image the higher the fusion frequency. This means that once again the cones perceive movement better than the rods and that light adaptation is an advantage.

In animal experiments fusion frequency can be measured in two ways. In one the animal is trained to react to a slowly rotating sectored disc but to ignore one that is uniform whether rotating or stationary. The sectored disc is then turned faster and faster until the point at which the animal no longer reacts to it is reached. The speed of rotation at this point represents the fusion frequency. This method has been used in the Siamese fighting fish [21], in the turtle

[54], in one of the geckos [53] and in the rat [118]. Not all animals are intelligent or amenable enough for training experiments to be possible and in any case the technique is tedious and time-consuming. In these cases use can often be made of the optomotor reaction. If an animal is placed within a hollow rotating cylinder painted with black and white vertical stripes it will turn its eyes, its head or its whole body in the direction of movement in an effort to keep the visual image stationary on the retina. When the cylinder rotates so fast that fusion ensues the movement will cease. This method has also been used to investigate colour vision. In such experiments the vertical stripes are painted in two different colours, the idea being that if the colours look alike to the animal there will be no optomotor reaction. As a means for the evaluation of colour vision this method has been severely criticized and, as we shall see in the next chapter, the results should probably be interpreted with caution.

The other method of measuring flicker-fusion frequency is by means of the electroretinogram. With intermittent stimulation it is easy to find the frequency at which the electrical responses become fused (Chapter 2, Figure 8). Several species have been investigated in this way, among them two nocturnal geckos [72], the guinea-pig [77], the rabbit [74], various squirrels and ground squirrels [34, 183] and the pigeon [77].

The faster an animal moves the better its perception of movement needs to be. This was found to be the case in insects where the flicker-fusion frequency (measured by the electroretinogram) was much higher in flying species. In the blowfly the fusion frequency was 100 cycles per second under conditions where it is only 40 cycles per second in man, and it can go up as high as 280 cycles per second if the intensity of the intermittent stimulus is increased [10]. In bees the fusion frequency can reach over 300 cycles per second under optimal conditions [12]. In contrast, the fusion frequency for the cricket, which cannot fly, is only 45 cycles per second under conditions where that of the blowfly is 156 cycles per second (11). At moderate intensities the flicker-fusion frequency for the human fovea in light adaptation is about 50 cycles per second while that for the peripheral retina is only 20 cycles per second. This finding illustrates the difference in the speed of response of the rods and the cones. The pure-rod retina of the guinea-pig shows a maximum fusion frequency of 45 to 50 cycles per second [77] at maximum intensity, while in the pure-cone retina of the ground squirrels the figure is over 100 cycles per second [34, 183].

We see that some perception of movement is vital to all the vertebrates and that this faculty is better developed for the cones than for the rods. The cones are superior partly because they are associated with smaller receptive fields and partly because they have quicker reactions so that the persistence time of vision is shorter, the effect of a discrete retinal stimulation does not linger so long. This means that a moving object that can be well differentiated by a cone retina, or by the pure-cone fovea, may only produce the sensation of an elongated blur for an animal with a rod retina. However, movement as such, though not its details, is well recognized by a rod retina or by a rod-dominated peripheral retina. This seems to be because movement is often of extreme importance and has great attention value, particularly when it affects a retina which is capable of little else in the way of visual performance. A vague movement caught out of the corner of the eye impels one to turn so as to bring the image, whatever it may represent, on to the fovea for more detailed examination.

10. Colour Vision

Colour vision is the faculty for distinguishing between the different wave-lengths that make up the visible spectrum independently of their respective brightnesses. It has been estimated that, under optimal conditions, the human eye with normal colour vision could probably distinguish up to 1,500 different hues in the visible spectrum which embraces the wave-lengths between 400 mμ at the blue end to about 800 mμ at the red. If we include the various purples which can be made by mixing the short and long wave-lengths in different proportions, the number of distinguishable hues is greatly increased; and if to this figure there are added all the hues that can be produced by mixing different wave-lengths in various proportions as well as the shades that are the result of adding white to (or desaturating) them the number is enormously greater.

If 1,500 hues can be distinguished in a range of 400 mμ, it follows that in some parts of the spectrum the human eye can differentiate between wave-lengths that are between 0·2 and 0·3 mμ apart. In the yellow part of the spectrum, where hue discrimination is best, competent authorities believe that the smallest step may be only 0·1 mμ. The main problem in colour vision is, therefore, that of the mechanism whereby this astounding feat is accomplished.

Colour vision in man, and apparently in animals too, is associated with the cones. It is best developed in the fovea and although the periphery of the human retina is not colour blind, as is sometimes stated, it requires greater intensities of stimulation than the fovea if colour differences are to be satisfactorily appreciated. In addition, night vision, which is mediated by the rods, is colourless vision. This appears to be because all our rods contain the same visual pigment and the reactions of a single pigment by itself can never produce a true wave-length differentiation. Figure 15 may make this clear. Here the curve represents the spectral sensitivity of the human rod

85

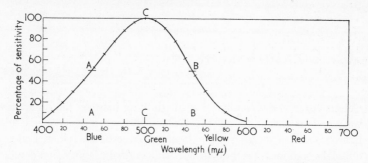

FIG. 15. Assumed spectral sensitivity of the mammalian rod visual pigment. With a single pigment such as this hue discrimination is impossible.

visual pigment and therefore of the end-organs containing it. In a homogeneous population of such end-organs stimulation by equal amounts of wave-length *A* and of wave-length *B* would produce exactly the same nervous effect and the two would, therefore, be indistinguishable. Also if one were to double the intensities of *A* and *B* the result would be a proportional increase in the effect and therefore the same as if stimulation were with wave-length *C* at the original intensity. In fact the effect of any spectral stimulus could be exactly matched merely by adjusting the intensity of any other one might care to choose. It would be impossible to distinguish change of intensity from change of hue. This is exactly what happens in night vision and in total colour blindness where a subject can match any part of the spectrum by using one wave-length and altering its intensity.

If, however, we have two sets of visual cells with different spectral sensitivities we do get a condition in which wave-length discrimination is possible. In Figure 16 the two curves represent the spectral sensitivities of two imaginary sets of visual end-organs. In this case stimulation by equal intensities of wave-lengths *A* and *B* would have very different results. Wave-length *A* would stimulate the first receptor but not the second, while wave-length *B* would stimulate the second but not the first. In addition, it would be impossible to match stimulation by wave-length *C* (which would affect both receptors equally) by any intensity of any other wave-length. To match C in this situation a mixture of two wave-lengths from the ends of the spectrum would be necessary. The situation in Figure 16 is a purely imaginary one invented to illustrate the minimum requirement for any sort of wave-length discrimination based on the spectral sensitivities of photosensitive pigments. It follows that in the human retina there is more than one type of cone and these different types must have different spectral sensitivities.

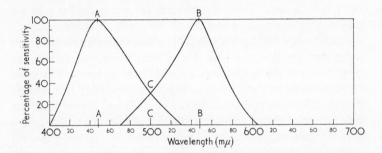

FIG. 16. The minimum requirement for hue discrimination. Spectral sensitivity curves of two imaginary visual pigments covering the same part of the spectrum as the curve of Figure 15, but giving a possibility of hue discrimination.

How many types of cone are necessary on such a hypothesis to explain the characteristics of human colour vision? Are two types enough or must we postulate many, perhaps one for each recognizably different hue in the spectrum? Or is a more likely number somewhere between these two extremes? In order to get an answer to this important question we must examine the results of experiments on colour vision. These have been of two kinds; there are those which are concerned with the sensations aroused by stimulating the eye by various wave-lengths and combinations of wave-lengths and those in which the responses of various parts of the visual apparatus to different coloured stimuli are studied. The first type of experiment is naturally most often done on human subjects who can describe their sensations, although properly controlled training experiments on suitable animals can tell one a great deal about their colour vision especially in the light of the human results.

Any theory of colour vision has to take into account, among other things, the sensations produced by mixing lights of different colour. At this point it must be emphasized that, since the stimulus to the eye is light, when one speaks of colour mixing in this context one always means mixtures of coloured lights and not of coloured pigments as used in painting. The results are very far from being the same in both cases. Thus, if one mixes red and green lights in the right proportions one gets a yellow. White can be produced by mixing blue and yellow and from this it follows that the right mixture of red and green (giving yellow) with blue can give white. But, in addition, every colour in the spectrum and out of it can be matched by some mixture of these three colours, although sometimes two will be enough. The colours that can be used in pairs to produce white are called complementary colours. Red and green (in fact a blue-green) are complementary and so are blue and yellow. In fact every spectral colour has a complementary somewhere in the spectrum or among the purples.

Any colour can be matched by some mixture of red, green and blue, three spectral colours. Two are not always enough. More than three colours are unnecessary. This at once suggests three mechanisms, probably three kinds of cone containing three different visual pigments and, therefore, with three different spectral sensitivity curves. What these sensitivity curves actually are we still do not know for certain, but one of the more recent suggestions is shown in Figure 17 [187]. This is the basis of the trichromatic theory which was first hinted at in the eighteenth century, accepted by Thomas Young in 1807 [227] and popularized by Helmholtz in 1867 [103]. This theory has not been allowed to pass uncriticized and it is not easy to explain all the facts of normal and defective human colour vision by means of it, nor all the results of animal experiments. It certainly does not represent the whole truth, but any complete theory of colour vision must embrace the undoubted trichromasy revealed by colour mixture.

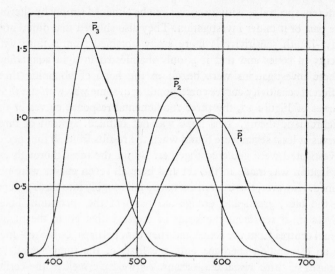

FIG. 17. Suggested fundamental response curves for three retinal mechanisms based on the results of colour mixing [187].

As we saw in Chapter 3 there is evidence of the presence of at least two visual pigments in the cones of the human fovea. One of these has its apparent maximum absorption at 540 mμ in the green part of the spectrum. The difference curve of this pigment is very similar to the central of the three postulated sensitivity curves shown in Figure 17 and also to that measured in the pure-cone retina of the grey squirrel. The second pigment has its maximum difference at 590 mμ which is also reminiscent of one of the curves of Figure 17. So far a blue-sensitive pigment that could account for the left-hand curve of Figure 17 has not been reported.

The results obtained with microelectrode recording from the retinal ganglion cells of several vertebrate species when coloured stimuli were used were briefly referred to in Chapter 2. One very important result of these experiments was to confirm, what had before been assumed theoretically, that the retina does possess means of analysing light in terms of its wave-length, in other words that

G

different spectral sensitivity curves can be obtained simply by altering the part of it under investigation. They also showed that differential wave-length sensitivity is more easily obtained from retinae with plenty of cones and that it is only manifested in light adaptation. These investigations were begun in the hope of obtaining three different sensitivity curves corresponding in some way with the three curves of Figure 17, the three fundamental response curves of the trichromatic theory. This hope was not fulfilled. Instead of three curves at least seven were found when the results from all the species investigated were gathered together. By far the most thorough examination was made in the cat and here all seven curves were obtained. However, these seven curves do fall roughly into three groups, in the blue, green and orange-red parts of the spectrum. These curves must represent the kinds of message that go to the higher visual centres from the retina and they can, perhaps, be looked upon as an elaboration (perhaps only the first) of the fundamental responses of three visual end-organs. As we have seen in the earlier chapters, the retina is a highly complex nervous structure containing many cross-connexions and, in most of the animals used in these experiments, there is no reason to believe that the responses of a single ganglion cell or optic nerve fibre reflect the uncomplicated response of a single end-organ.

The trichromatic theory provides a satisfactory explanation of the colour mixture data; it can also be used to explain many of the forms of colour blindness in man and some other aspects of colour vision [224]. There are, however, phenomena such as colour contrast and some experimental results with colour adaptation which are not satisfactorily covered by this theory in any simple way. Such difficulties have led to the formulation of numerous other colour vision theories designed to overcome them. Unfortunately most of these theories take no account of the unquestionable trichromasy of human colour vision and are, therefore, not acceptable.

The most successful of these alternatives has been the opponent colours theory of Hering [104]. This theory is based on the psychological purity of black, white, blue, green, yellow and red. Every other hue appears to our consciousness as some mixture of these sensations. These six sensations can be divided into three opponent pairs, white and black, yellow and blue, red and green. Hering suggested three retinal substances, the breakdown of one of which produced the first sensation of each pair while its synthesis produced the second. This conception of psychologically 'pure' sensations being necessarily the direct result of fundamental physiological mechanisms is not really very satisfactory. We know that two of Hering's 'pure' sensations, yellow and white, can, in fact, be produced by mixed stimuli apparently activating at least two retinal mechanisms at the same time. Further, the idea of breakdown and synthesis of chemical substances in the receptors being responsible for different sensations does not fit easily into modern theories of nerve stimulation. All the same, the notion of opponent mechanisms does go far to explain many colour phenomena which are hard to understand on the basis of the trichromatic theory and that alone.

In addition, the results of some of the investigations of the electrical responses of the retina to stimulation by light seem to point directly to a system of opponent reactions. First of all black does appear to be a definite sensation, not just the result of a complete absence of any stimulus. Many retinal ganglion cells show an 'off-response' which, one would suppose, must convey a positive message to the brain. This off-response is thought to be associated with inhibitory activity in the retina [93]. Then there is much evidence of a mechanism which signals changes in brightness (whiteness) and which is independent of the retinal colour mechanisms [93, 115]. Lastly there is some work in which the responses from within the retinae of several species of fish have been investigated using differently coloured light simuli [134, 178]. Here again there was evidence of an independent brightness mechanism with a broad spectral sensitivity curve covering most of the visible spectrum. There were also other responses grouped in two pairs, yellow-blue and red-green. These responses took the form of a series of steady potential changes of opposite sign, usually negative following yellow or red stimuli and positive for blue or green. The responses were not recorded from the cones themselves but from a level embracing the cone synapses and the horizontal cells. It is not at all clear how these responses are related to those which can be recorded from the ganglion cells, but they do strongly suggest a set of opponent retinal mechanisms.

The phenomenon of simultaneous contrast has always been one of the most difficult to explain by means of the trichromatic theory. If a small patch of colour is viewed against a neutral background it soon appears to be surrounded by a ring of the opponent or complementary colour. Also if the patch is black or white its immediate surround will appear lighter or darker. Hering explained these observations by assuming that a breakdown or synthesis of colour-mediating substance induced the opposite reaction in the surrounding retina. We now know that retinal interaction does indeed take place although the interaction is usually electrical. We saw in Chapter 2 that stimulation of the immediate surroundings of the receptive field of an individual ganglion cell inhibits the response of its centre. This finding immediately suggests a possible mechanism for simultaneous contrast, in any case between black and white. The experiments have not been done with coloured stimuli. It appears, therefore, that the opponent sensations may well be due not to the breakdown and synthesis of chemical substances but to an interplay of nervous excitation and inhibition.

There is no doubt that colour vision in man is fundamentally trichromatic but it also seems necessary to accept a thesis of opponent mechanisms in some form or other. It now seems most probable that the three fundamental mechanisms will turn out to be three photopigments with different spectral-sensitivity curves situated in the retinal cones, and that the opponent reactions are the result of an elaboration, probably by means of excitations and inhibitions, of their responses. Some of this elaboration appears to take place in the retina but more may well occur at the cell stations between the retina and the cortex where the colour messages are finally received.

It is not always easy to be sure whether or not an animal possesses colour vision. Sometimes it is possible to come to a decision on the basis of an animal's normal behaviour. Where colour is a feature of only one sex, as is so often the case in birds, or is used in mating or threat displays it is likely that the species in question can distinguish hue. This is the case in the robin, for instance, where it has been shown that a territory-holding male attacks another intruding male because of its red breast. Immature males do not have the red breast and are not attacked. A stuffed immature robin was not attacked, while a mere bunch of red feathers which did not look at all like a bird, let alone a robin, was attacked [124]. Similar observations in which the reactions of fish and birds to coloured and to colourless models of bizarre shape have shown that the red belly of a territory-invading male stickleback is the stimulus which incites the male in occupation to attack and that it is the red spot on the bill of the parent herring-gull which causes pecking in the hungry chick [189]. However, where colour is not a prominent feature of an animal's normal environment other methods have to be employed.

The possession of a retinal mechanism for analysing wave-length differences apparently does not necessarily mean that the owner of the retina has colour vision. Thus some differential wave-length sensitivity has been demonstrated in the cat [92], the rat [88] and the guinea-pig [90] but behaviour experiments indicate that neither the cat [49, 99], the rat [211] nor the guinea-pig has colour vision.

The most satisfactory method of discovering whether or not an animal has true colour vision is by training experiments. These are tedious and time-consuming and it is very important that they be properly controlled. It must be established beyond all doubt that the animal under training is making its discriminations on the basis of hue alone and that other cues such as smell, hearing, touch or a sense of position are not being employed. It is also vital to know that the animal's choice is not really on the basis of brightness instead of colour. If an animal is trained to go to a green target and to avoid a red one it is necessary to adjust the intensities of the two stimuli so that they appear equally bright to the animal. In order to do this a knowledge of its spectral sensitivity curve is necessary. If the green and red stimuli are of equal physical intensity the red one will usually appear darker to an animal because its retina is less sensitive to the long wave-lengths. It is not even enough to equate the intensities so that they look equally bright to the human eye, for the animal's spectral sensitivity curve is not necessarily the same as the human one. It is desirable to establish the spectral sensitivity curve before proceeding to test hue discrimination. This can be done by training positive to the brighter of two targets after which it is relatively easy to establish which parts of the spectrum look brighter and which darker by exposing different coloured stimuli in pairs. It is then possible to train to a target of a given colour and to match this with various others so that they will appear equally bright to the animal in question. By this means it will be possible to determine whether there is discrimination on the basis of hue alone and, depending on how many colours are tested, get some idea of the efficiency of hue discrimination throughout the spectrum. Such elaborate experiments are rarely done. It is more usual to train the experimental animal to a given colour and then to present this colour paired with a series of greys ranging from black to white. If enough greys are used in the range and the animal always makes the correct choice it is almost certain that this choice is made on the basis of hue and not on the basis of brightness. The animal has colour vision.

Training experiments are usually only possible in animals of relatively high intelligence and which will become sufficiently tame to be trained. In cases where this is not easy or even possible, use has been made of the optomotor reaction as was mentioned in the last chapter. For such experiments a hollow rotating cylinder is painted inside with vertical stripes of two alternate colours or of one colour and a grey. If two colours are used, it is necessary once again to know the spectral sensitivity curve so that the colours may be equated in brightness for the animal. This method has been severely criticized [208] on the grounds that it will be so difficult as to be virtually impossible to get an absolute equation between the brightness of the stripes and that this will suggest colour vision where there is actually none. If there is no optomotor reaction the inference is that the alternating stripes look identical to the animal. When the optomotor reaction is used negative results may be more reliable than positive ones.

Another method which has been used is to colour the animal's food, either by dyeing or by illumination with coloured lights, and to see which colour it seems to prefer. There are several objections to this procedure. There is absolutely no way of knowing whether the choice is made on the basis of brightness or of hue and the animal may ignore one colour not because he can't see it but because food is never that colour in nature. Erroneous conclusions were reached about the hen's sensitivity to blue light as a result of using this method. Grain was illuminated with spectral lights and it was found that the seeds lying under the blue end of the spectrum were not taken. It was concluded that the hen's eye is not sensitive to blue because they apparently could not see the blue seed [108]. Later work in which hens were trained to differently coloured grains showed that they are sensitive to blue after all [208].

Some workers believe that if an animal shows a Purkinje shift (see Chapter 2) it must, therefore, have colour vision. Their argument assumes that cone vision is always coloured vision. Although it is true that colour vision appears always to be associated with cones and light adaptation we do not *know* that all predominantly cone eyes possess colour vision. A Purkinje shift only demonstrates that the retina in question possesses two types of visual cell with different spectral sensitivity curves, one used predominantly in the light-adapted state, the other in the dark-adapted state. It proves nothing either way about whether colour vision is present or not. Some pure-cone eyes, which will show no Purkinje shift, may well have colour vision.

There has been a vast amount of work on colour vision in animals although many of the earlier experiments are useless because brightness was not properly controlled. So far as fishes are concerned no species properly investigated has been shown to be colour blind, and the evidence for colour vision in some is very good. The most extensive work has been done on *Phoxinus laevis* and on the stickleback, *Gasterosteus aculeatus*. The former apparently has trichromatic vision and for it mixtures of the human complementary colours yellow and blue, red and blue-green and orange and blue-violet are seen as white [100]. The existence of complementary colours like those for man has also been shown in the Siamese fighting fish [21]. It seems probable that all cone-rich teleosts have colour vision and many of them show highly-coloured markings. Some fish react vigorously to particular colours, especially red and blue, but it is not known how important colour may be to them in their natural surroundings. They may also be very sensitive to intensity changes [166] and form seems to be important too, at least to the carp [112].

Most of the work on colour vision in amphibia has been by means of the optomotor reaction. Frog (*Rana temporaria*) tadpoles gave negative results [25] while the adult frogs could apparently distinguish red and blue as distinct hues [24]. Good colour vision has been claimed for six species of Urodela by this method, but complete colour blindness was found in three species of toad [24]. This last finding was confirmed by training experiments for two of the same species [185]. Recent experiments both on the electrical responses of the frog (*Rana pipiens*) diencephalon [145] and on the positive phototactic response of the same species [146], and of *Rana temporaria* [147] suggest that frogs have at least a mechanism for the appreciation of blue as a separate sensation. It is suggested that the retinal endorgans responsible are the green rods [63], since amphibian species without these particular visual cells do not show positive phototaxis [148].

Among the reptiles no work has been done on snakes and we do not know at all whether or not they have colour vision. Training experiments on two species of alligator have been claimed to demonstrate a 'weak' colour vision but the results are not really convincing [154]. These species are nocturnal and have a predominantly rod retina although cones are present.

The tortoises and turtles probably all have colour vision. Training experiments have shown that three tortoise and one turtle species can distinguish different hues from one another and from a series of greys [122, 164, 165]. In the case of one tortoise, *Emys europaea*, and the turtle, *Clemmys caspica*, the best discrimination was in the orange part of the spectrum [221] whereas in man it is in the yellow. This may be connected with the fact that the tortoise (*Testudo graeca*) spectral sensitivity curve has its maximum in the orange (600 mμ). This spectral sensitivity curve was measured electrically [89]. The maximum of the human photopic curve is in the yellow at about 560 mμ.

The lizards also have pure-cone retinae and those which have been tested appear to have colour vision. *Lacerta agilis* was studied by training with coloured mealworms, precautions being taken to ensure that the choice was made on the basis of vision and not of taste or smell [196]. The optomotor reaction was used on *Anolis carolinensis* and the slow-worm both of which are claimed to discriminate hues [151]. When the same method was tried with two species of nocturnal gecko, *Hemidactylus turcicus* and *Tarentola mauritanica*, the results were entirely negative. These geckos have pure-rod retinae while the lizards have only cones.

No one seriously questions that the diurnal birds have colour vision. We have already seen that herring-gull chicks react specifically to the red spot on the parents' bill and it is known that budgerigars recognize the sex of their companions by the colour of their ceres. The male has a blue cere, the female a brown one and it has been shown that males will attack a female whose cere is painted blue and court a male whose cere is painted brown [45]. Most of the work on avian colour vision has been done on the domestic fowl. This has been shown by entirely satisfactory behaviour experiments to have hue discrimination very like that of man [125]. This bird appears to enjoy trichromatic vision; it can also experience simultaneous contrast [167]. Trichromatic vision has also been demonstrated in the pigeon [101]. It is not certain what effect the coloured oil droplets in the cones of the bird retina would have on its hue discrimination. Since the droplets, red, orange and yellow, preferentially absorb the short wave-lengths of the spectrum, birds are likely to be less good at discriminating the blue colours than we are. However this does not seem to be true of the hen and pigeon. Except for the budgerigar which is said to have no red oil droplets [160], those birds which have been tested show some insensitivity at the blue end of the spectrum.

All birds have both rods and cones in their retinae but the proportions are very different between diurnal and nocturnal species. It is not known whether strictly nocturnal birds have any colour vision. However, the little owl, which is not truly nocturnal, was tested by training experiments with coloured papers matched against a grey series [139]. Yellow, green and blue were distinguished from all the greys but it was doubtful whether red could be told from the darkest grey.

On the whole, mammals appear not to have colour vision except for the primates where it is well developed and almost certainly trichromatic [22, 46]. An exception is the lemur which is apparently colour blind [23]. The tree shrew, said to have a pure-cone retina, and which is strongly diurnal, could distinguish red, yellow, green and blue papers from sixty-two shades of grey between black and white [188]. When the illumination was lowered this discrimination was no longer possible. Most mammals have rod-dominated retinae and some have pure-rod ones. The house mouse [121], the long-tailed field mouse [173], the rat [47, 211], the guinea-pig [141], the rabbit [210], the racoon [140], the opossum [173], the polecat [143] and the cat [49, 99] have all been shown to be colour blind, although some workers have claimed a poor colour sense for the last [33]. It seems probable that the cat does not, in any case, use colour vision in normal life, for the discriminations were very hard to establish and were very easily lost [32]. Some colour vision has been suggested for ungulates [13, 14], but the experiments are not very satisfactory. A very 'weak' colour vision may possibly be present in dogs [49, 174] but this has been denied by other workers [95].

The interesting mammals from the point of view of colour vision are those with pure-cone retinae. There have been several investigations on various squirrel species and none has shown a really well-developed colour sense, although all indicate some hue discrimination. The species examined were the red squirrel [130, 138, 173], the American red squirrel [49] and the souslik or European ground squirrel [30, 121].

It would be interesting to know whether animal colour vision is always trichromatic or whether there are other less complicated forms. Granit's work on the retinal colour-sensitivity curves of a good selection of species suggests that even, as in the cat, where an animal can apparently not use its colour mechanisms there are still three present in the retina. Attempts to decide the type of colour vision present have only been made on two fish, the hen, the pigeon and some primates. It seems likely that where colour vision is well developed as in teleost fish, most reptiles, birds and the primates, it is always trichromatic; but what types of mechanism are present in animals said to have 'weak' colour vision is not known. If truly present in such mammals as the dog and the ungulates it is possibly trichromatic but much diluted by the colourless reactions of the dominant rods of the retina. The situation in the squirrels is very puzzling. Although all investigators have been able to train these pure-cone species to discriminate hue none has found it an easy task. Some [30] have found their animals to use brightness in preference to colour while others [130] report that colour vision was 'rudimentary'. By this they mean that only a few hues could be distinguished. No squirrel was able to tell red from dark grey and some couldn't tell blue or green from grey either. Yellow presented the least difficulty. It is possible that the squirrels have only two retinal mechanisms for hue discrimination instead of the more usual three. The squirrel spectral sensitivity curve shows an insensitivity to red and two maxima in the green and blue [184]. The green part of the curve matches the difference curve for the squirrel retinal pigment [215] as well as that for the human foveal pigment thought to mediate the green retinal mechanism [172]. The squirrel, therefore, would appear to possess the green mechanism and perhaps also a blue one but it would seem most unlikely, in view of the behaviour results and the spectral sensitivity curve, that it should have a red mechanism anything like ours.

11. Adaptation to Various Habitats

There is no doubt that the vertebrate eye originated in the water, so that most of the adaptations it has undergone in response to changes in habitat are those necessary to protect it from desiccation on transfer to the land and those required for aerial as opposed to aquatic vision.

The eye retains its global shape because of the intra-ocular pressure. This is maintained because there is a balance between the production of aqueous humour and its drainage from the eye. In most animals the aqueous humour is produced by secretion from the epithelial cells of the processes of the ciliary body. It is drained away into the blood through the aqueous veins and the canal of Schlemn. In lampreys and fish there is no ciliary body and, therefore, there are no special secretory cells. It is not known how, or from whence, the aqueous humour is produced in these eyes. In freshwater forms water might enter the eye by osmosis through the cornea, the correct pressure being maintained by controlled drainage. The elasmobranchs have a high level of urea in their blood so that its osmotic pressure is above that of sea-water and in some, at least, the osmotic pressure of the intra-ocular fluids is higher still so that osmosis might be sufficient to maintain the necessary volume of aqueous humour and so the intra-ocular pressure. It is awkward for this hypothesis that the elasmobranchs are the only fish to have anything resembling ciliary processes. There are no consistent anatomical differences between the eyes of fresh-water and marine teleosts, and if the fresh-water species control their intra-ocular pressure by means of osmosis how do the marine species do it? Also there are the anadromous (salmon and trout) and catadromous (eels, some lampreys) species which move from fresh water to salt and vice versa and whose eyes show no changes which could be referred to secretory activity at the time of the transfer.

One characteristic of water is that it absorbs light, some wave-lengths more than others. Because of suspended organic matter, mostly yellow in colour, the water of rivers, lakes and ponds absorbs the short wave-lengths of light more than the long. This may be the reason why the dominant visual pigment of fresh-water fish usually has its maximum absorption in the green part of the spectrum while that of land animals and marine fish absorbs maximally at a shorter wave-length in the blue-green. Clear sea water absorbs the long wave-lengths more than the short and the pigments of deep-sea fish tend to have their maxima at even shorter wave-lengths in the blue. These points have already been discussed in Chapter 3. Fish which live deeper in the sea, where there is little light, have more pigment in their rods whose outer segments are lengthened, thereby increasing the chances of catching light quanta.

Very deep-sea fish which live at depths where there is no natural daylight but where there are luminous organisms and the fish themselves have photopohores, either have much reduced eyes or have relatively enormous ones showing all the usual nocturnal characteristics (Chapter 4). The cones have been eliminated from the retina and the rods much increased in number and length. In some deep-sea teleosts the retino-motor reactions have disappeared and the pigment epithelium may even be completely devoid of pigment. The eyes have increased in size and may be tubular while the lens has become very large. Sometimes the iris even has been dispensed with. The eyes are often frontally placed and this probably helps to increase the over-all visual sensitivity [216]. Fish depend greatly on senses other than vision, especially on the reception of chemical stimuli and of vibrations transmitted through the water. In consequence, blinding is not so catastrophic in fish as it is in many terrestrial species. So a number of species which live on the bottom and are nocturnal have much reduced eyes and some which have taken to living in caves have lost their eyes altogether. Such fish can retain some sensitivity to light, apparently through the skin [123] although it is not obvious whether they make any use of it.

Because the refractive power of the cornea is eliminated under water the lens is the most important refracting structure in the fish eye. In consequence, fish eyes often project so far from the head that the lens itself sticks out. This much increases the size of the visual field. In other fish the eyes do not project and in these cases stream-lining is improved at the expense of the visual field. To assist in stream-lining, the fish eye is flattened so that its shortest diameter coincides with the visual axis. The cornea is flattened too and it is often thickened towards the rim so that it has added strength to resist the water currents produced by swimming. The sclera is cartilaginous and may be calcified. In addition, many fish have scleral ossicles and these are best developed in the swiftest swimming species such as the tunny and swordfish. These scleral ossicles are not related to those of reptiles and birds which are developed to resist the pull of the intra-ocular muscles during accommodation (Chapter 7), in fish they are useful in combating distortion due to water pressure. Many fish have vertical eyelids and in some the aperture between them has been obliterated and a type of spectacle has been developed. We shall discuss the development of spectacles a little later. Some fish through living on the bottom have developed into flatfish. They are virtually lying on their sides and in this position the lower eye has migrated to the top of the head so that the fish has an upward-looking field of view. This has happened in the soles, plaice and flounders.

When animals took their eyes out of water they developed glands in the orbit and along the eyelids some of which, the lachrimal glands, secrete watery tears while others, such as the Harderian gland, produce an oily secretion. These secretions irrigate the cornea, washing and lubricating it, and helping to protect it from desiccation and other damage. When the marine aquatic mammals returned to the water they needed some extra protection for the cornea. In these mammals, the dugongs, manatees, whales and seals the Harderian gland is much enlarged and an abundant oily secretion is produced which protects the exposed parts of the eye from both salt and water. Dugongs and manatees have not otherwise altered the structure of the eye from the terrestrial type and, in consequence, they have very poor underwater vision, depending on their highly-developed sense of smell. Whale eyes are flattened like fish eyes and have a similar cornea thickened round the rim. The lens is also like that of a fish in being nearly spherical and having a high refractive index. Seal eyes are also somewhat flattened and again the lens is nearly spherical. The seal cornea is astigmatic having a shorter radius of curvature in the horizontal meridian. This does not matter under water where vision should be quite good with the fishlike eye.

The pupil dilates to a very large circle under water but closes to a tiny vertical slit when the seal comes out into the brighter light ashore. This little slit cuts out the corneal irregularities and acts as a stenopaeic aperture to give good focusing power in the air. A pupil as large as the seal's when dilated could not close to a pinhole.

The big change in the vertebrate eye during evolution came when animals left the water for the land. One important problem was to protect the cornea, which now became the main refracting structure, from damage and desiccation. We have seen that protection from desiccation was partially achieved by secretions from glands in the orbit and adnexa. In addition, mobile eyelids appeared and these by their reflex blinking help to protect the cornea from damage by foreign bodies. A 'third eyelid', the nictitating membrane, is also present in many species. This has evolved as a fold in the conjunctiva at the nasal corner of the lid opening. In reptiles and birds the nictitating membrane has its associated muscles which can draw it across the front of the eyeball. In mammals there is no such musculature and the movement is a passive one, the nictitating membrane slips across the cornea when the eye is withdrawn somewhat into the orbit. In reptiles and in birds, except the owls and dippers, the nictitating membrane is transparent so that it does not interfere with vision when covering the cornea. Many ornithologists believe that the avian nictitating membrane permanently covers the cornea while a bird is in flight and so prevents desiccation by air currents. On the whole the nictitating membrane is least well developed in the lower mammals although it is absent in man and the primates. In an animal such as the horse the nictitating membrane may protect the eye from foreign bodies in the environment when it lowers its head among the grass to graze.

The best method of protecting an eye from foreign bodies is by the development of a spectacle. These may be of three kinds. A primary spectacle is formed by a modification of the skin over the eye so that it provides a transparent covering. This is the type present in the lampreys. A secondary spectacle, which is a feature of practically all amphibious fish and of those fish which grope for food on a sandy or muddy bottom, is produced by an actual fusion between the over-lying skin and the cornea. Some teleost fish with protuberant eyes also have a secondary spectacle, presumably to protect the cornea from the water currents set up by swimming. In snakes and some burrowing and desert-living lizards a tertiary spectacle is developed by a fusion of the eyelids and a subsequent modification of the tissue to render it transparent. In these species the spectacle is shed with the skin, and this renewal is very necessary for the spectacle may become so obviously scratched and abraded by particles of sand and grit that it has sometimes been thought that snakes go blind before changing their skins. The usefulness of a spectacle to a burrowing animal is obvious for this habit will otherwise put the eyes in constant danger. Some moles have the lid opening constricted to vanishing-point but these have developed no transparent spectacle and the eye beneath the skin is vestigial. A spectacle is also present in some nocturnal lizards such as the geckos. It has been suggested that this is because such small nocturnal animals could not see obstacles such as gravel or stubble and needed more protection for the eye than is given by lids [204], but no small nocturnal mammal has developed a spectacle. Some geckos are diurnal and these also have a spectacle; this, among other ocular features, is thought to show that they have evolved from nocturnal ancestors [204, 191] and have become secondarily diurnal. Most snakes are diurnal and although their eyes are usually near the ground, so are those of the diurnal lizards which have no spectacles, whereas all snakes show this feature. The snake spectacle is an indi-cation that these species have passed through a phase of underground living [204]. Any animal which can shed its skin periodically, and thus renew its spectacle, is better off with one than with eyelids. But the tertiary spectacle only appears to have developed in the reptiles in response to burrowing and perhaps other habits which present great danger to the eyes. A few teleost fish have tertiary spectacles formed by fusion of the vertical lids. Tertiary spectacles are only found in swift-swimming species; sluggish species, if they have spectacles at all, have evolved secondary ones.

Amphibious animals mostly achieve good vision both in water and in air, when they can do this at all, by increasing the range of accommodation (Chapter 7). But there are a few exceptions. The South American 'four-eyed fish', *Anableps*, swims on the surface with the eyes only half immersed. This fish has two pupils in each eye, one of which is normally above, the other below the water. The curvature of the lens is not uniform but is so arranged that the lower part, through which rays from under the water pass, is more highly curved than the upper part. Thus, this fish has simultaneously good underwater vision through its lower pupils and good aerial vision through its upper ones with no need for accommodation. Other more truly amphibious fish which spend much time at the surface or even completely out of water have the eyes adapted for aerial vision. These include certain gobies, among them the mud-skipper, *Periopthalmus*. *Periophthalmus* spends most of its time out of the water on mud flats exposed at low tide. Its eyes, which are highly mobile to compensate for its lack of a neck, are set in turrets and are protected from desiccation by secondary spectacles. They are not at all fishlike in their optics. Fish without spectacles which keep the eyes much out of water may be seen to dip the head periodically. This action would also serve to save the cornea from desiccation.

We have seen in Chapter 7 that certain aquatic birds, notably the cormorants and dippers, have enormous powers of accommodation which give them equally good vision both in the air and under the water. The diving ducks, loons and auks have better accommodation than land birds but it is not up to the standard of the cormorants and dippers. However, they have a nictitating membrane which is highly refractile, even in water, and which, when drawn across the cornea, increases the total power of the optical system of the eye. The diving ducks have a much thickened cornea which may be a help in withstanding the shock of immersion as well as being a support against the pull of the powerful accommodatory muscles. All diving birds have extra thick sclerae and especially heavy scleral ossicles. Crampton's muscle, which is a feature of the avian eye and which, when contracted, pulls on the cornea shortening its radius of curvature to help accommodation, is very insignificant, or sometimes completely absent, in underwater swimmers. There is no point in changing the corneal curvature under water, it can have no effect on accommodation. The kingfisher apparently has good vision in water as well as on land but this bird has no special accommodatory mechanism. It has however, got two foveae in each retina and the lenses are egg-shaped and arranged so that light reaching the temporal fovea has to pass through its more highly curved portion. It has been suggested [120] that the temporal foveae are used when the kingfisher is hunting under water and that the central foveae and less-curved part of the lens serve aerial vision.

Such amphibious animals as the crocodile and hippopotamus spend most of their time in the water, but their eyes are constructed for vision in the air. Here both eyes and nostrils are situated on top of the head so that they remain in the air while the rest of the body is submerged.

When in the course of evolution an animal emerges from the water it immediately receives more light and, unless it is to take up nocturnal habits, its eyes need to become less sensitive. So one finds that, on the whole, terrestrial eyes belonging to diurnal species have a preponderance of cones in the retina. In fact the rods may disappear altogether. No eye which is used under water has a pure-cone retina, while the elasmobranchs and some deep-sea teleosts have pure-rod ones. But most of the terrestrial reptiles have no rods at all and many diurnal birds have very few. The diving birds, however, always have a good number of rods to give better sensitivity under the reduced light conditions which obtain in the water. A mobile pupil also appears with terrestrial life and this further helps to protect the eyes from dazzle. Fish do not have mobile pupils and the retino-motor reactions, which have been replaced by the pupil reactions, are too sluggish to be quickly effective. Retino-motor reactions are to be found in amphibia and birds but they are still slow and, in birds at least, are probably reinforced by the rapid closure of the pupil.

12. What Do Animals Really See?

One can make some estimate of how good an animal's visual powers are likely to be by studying its eyes. An examination of its retina should tell us how acute its vision will probably be or whether visual acuity has been sacrificed to nocturnal sensitivity. The presence and state of development of its intra-ocular muscles should indicate the extent of its powers of accommodation, while the position of the eyes in the head gives one information about the size of its binocular visual field and, therefore, of its possibilities for stereoscopic vision. The expectations aroused by a study of an animal's eyes are often fulfilled by a study of its visual behaviour. Animals with many cones usually appear to have good visual acuity and colour vision, as, for instance, the diurnal lizards and birds, while those with many rods are usually nocturnal or inhabit places where the illumination is low. Those animals which display good vision both in air and water, such as some aquatic birds, give every indication of having a powerful accommodatory mechanism. Hunting animals, both birds and mammals, tend to have frontal eyes with large binocular fields which should give satisfactory stereoscopic vision and, therefore, accuracy in attacking.

However, animals may display visual powers greater than those that would be expected from the structure of their eyes. A pouncing cat apparently has good visual acuity, but its retina does not seem to be any better constructed from this point of view than our own peripheral retina whose visual acuity is known to be extremely poor. But human beings with grossly myopic eyes uncorrected by spectacles can sometimes, with special experience, be wonderfully successful at interpreting their blurred retinal images, and one-eyed people with no stereoscopic vision have been known to make good table tennis players.

On the other hand animals can behave as if objects were invisible

H*

under circumstances where excellent vision would be expected. We have already seen that cats have the retinal mechanism for colour vision but they are, apparently, colour blind. In this case the failure in colour vision may be in nervous structures central to the retina. A similar central defect has been suspected in completely colour blind human subjects with good cone vision [212]. In other cases the explanation appears to be that the animal simply does not pay attention to aspects of the visual scene which its eyes seem perfectly capable of recording. The male robin defending its territory against an invading bird is apparently uninterested in any part of the invader's appearance except his red breast. But the robin's eye has a structure both of the optical system and of the retina which should provide the bird with a clear picture of another robin in all its detail. Under certain circumstances nesting herring-gulls behave as though their eggs were invisible to them. If, in the gull's absence, the eggs are removed and put just outside the nest the parent bird will retrieve them, but if the distance is made a little greater the bird will sit happily on the empty nest with the eggs in full sight. That the eggs can be seen perfectly well is indicated by removing them still farther away, the gull will then eat them as it does its neighbour's eggs if it should find them unguarded [189]. Herring-gull chicks show camouflage colouring very similar to that of the eggs but the parent bird never has any difficulty in seeing and recognizing its own chicks. There is nothing wrong with the herring-gull's eyes. The explanation of the different reactions to eggs and chicks appears to be that, under normal circumstances, the eggs do not leave the nest and it is, therefore, sufficient if the parent knows the position of the nest, while the active chicks often wander away and have to be got back.

Numerous other instances of the same sort could be quoted. The territory-defending male stickleback is, like the robin in a similar situation, excited to attack an invader by the red colour of his enemy's throat and belly. The appearance of the rest of the fish is of no interest to him and he will attack anything which is red. This was shown by experiments using models when representations which did not look at all like a stickleback were attacked if the underside were painted red, but the fish took little interest in an accurate model if the red coloration were lacking [189]. It is even recorded that sticklebacks tried to attack the red mail vans passing along the road outside the laboratory window in front of which their tanks were placed. Herring-gull chicks when begging for food from the parent's bill are stimulated by the red spot on it, as more experiments with oddly shaped models have proved. The shape of the 'bill' in these experiments did not affect the chick's reaction if the red colour were present, but the position of the coloured patch in relation to the rest of the 'bill' was important [189].

It is not certain whether the widespread preference for moving prey is of the same nature or whether the stationary victim is truly invisible. It seems probable that the latter is the case where the prey is well camouflaged. We have all ourselves had the experience of having been unable to see an animal until it chanced to move. In some species movement seems necessary for a stimulus to be effective. Many of the individual cells in the rabbit's lateral geniculate nucleus do not respond readily to a stationary stimulus to the eye, but most respond well to a moving or flickering light [5].

In considering animal vision we have all the time to resist the assumption that because we know something about structures in the human eye ultimately responsible for sensations, such as colour and form, we can necessarily tell what an animal actually 'sees' from the structure and physiological reactions of its eyes. This assumption is particularly dangerous just because it is apparently so often correct. We have seen that in its general structure and particularly in the large number of rods present, the retina of a nocturnal animal resembles our own peripheral retina. And this, we know, is the part of our retina which is most sensitive to low illuminations at night. Again, those vertebrates which indubitably have colour vision tend to have a preponderance of cones just as does our fovea where hue discrimination is at its height. Perhaps it would be fair to say that a good knowledge of the anatomy and physiology of an animal's eye will tell us how much that eye is capable of as an optical instrument; it will not necessarily tell us what use the animal makes of it, or is, indeed, able to make of it. An imperfect apprehension of the sensory world of animals usually prevents our being able to speak confidently of what the 'vision' of a given species is really like. On the other hand familiarity with the structure and physiological reactions of its eyes, together with an understanding of its behaviour and requirements, can, perhaps, enable us to make not too foolish a guess.

References

[1] ADLER, H. E. and DALLAND, J. I. (1959). 'Spectral thresholds in the starling (*Sturnus vulgaris*).' *J. Comp. Physicl. Psychol.*, **52**, 438–45.

[2] ALI, M. A. (1962). 'Retinal responses in enucleated eyes of Atlantic salmon (*Salmo salar*).' *Rev. Canad. Biol.*, **21**, 7–15.

[3] ALTEVOGT, R. (1955). 'Das visuelle Minimum separabile eines indischen Elefanten.' *Z. vergleich. Physiol.*, **37**, 325–37.

[4] ARDEN, G. B. (1963). 'Complex receptive fields and responses to moving objects in cells of the rabbit's lateral geniculate body.' *J. Physiol.*, **166**, 468–88.

[5] ARDEN, G. B. and LIU, Y. M. (1960). 'Some types of response of single cells in the rabbit lateral geniculate body to stimulation of the retina by light and to electrical stimulation of the optic nerve.' *Acta physiol. scand.*, **48**, 36–48.

[6] ARDEN, G. B. and SILVER, P. H. (1962). 'Visual thresholds and spectral sensitivities of the grey squirrel (*Sciurus carolinensis leucotis*.)' *J. Physiol.*, **163**, 540–57.

[7] ARDEN. G. B. and TANSLEY. K. (1962). 'The electroretinogram of a diurnal gecko.' *J. gen. Physiol.*, **45**, 1145–61.

[8] ARDEN, G. B. and WEALE, R. A. (1954). 'Nervous mechanisms and dark adaptation.' *J. Physiol.*, **125**, 417–26.

[9] ARMINGTON, J. C. and THIEDE, F. C. (1956). 'Electroretinal demonstration of a Purkinje shift in the chicken eye.' *Amer. J. Physiol.*, **186**, 258–62.

[10] AUTRUM, H. (1948). Über das zeitliche Auflösungsvermögen des Insektenauges.' *Nach. Akad. Wiss. Göttingen. Math.-Phys. Kl.*, **2**, 8–12.

[11] AUTRUM, H. (1948). 'Zur Analyse des zeitlichen Auflösungsvermögen des Insektenauges.' *Nach. Akad. Wiss. Göttingen Math.-Phys. Kl.*, **2**, 13–18.

[12] AUTRUM, H. and STÖCKER, M. (1950). 'Die Verschemelzungsfrequenzen des Bienenauges.' *Z. Naturforsch.*, **5b**, 38–43.

[13] BACKHAUS, D. (1959). 'Experimentelle Untersuchungen über die Sehschärfe und das Farbensehen einiger Huftiere.' *Z. Tierpsychol.*, **16**, 445–67.

[14] BACKHAUS, D. (1959). 'Experimentelle Prüfung des Farbseh-vermögens einer Massai-Giraffe (*Giraffa camelopardalis tippelskir-chi*, Matschie 1898).' *Z. Tierpsychol.*, **16**, 468–77.

[15] BALL, S., GOODWIN, T. W. and MORTON, R. A. (1948). 'Studies on vitamin A. 5. The preparation of retinene-vitamin A aldehyde.' *Biochem. J.*, **42**, 516–23.

[16] BARLOW, H. B. (1953). 'Summation and inhibition in the frog's retina.' *J. Physiol.*, **119**, 69–88.

[17] BARLOW, H. B., FITZHUGH, R. and KUFFLER, S. W. (1957). 'Change of organization in the receptive fields of the cat's retina during dark adaptation.' *J. Physiol.*, **137**, 338–54.

[18] BARLOW, H. B. and HILL, R. M. (1963). 'Selective sensitivity to direction of movement in ganglion cell of the rabbit retina.' *Science*, **139**, 412–14.

[19] BAYLOR, E. R. and SHAW, E. (1962). 'Refractive error and vision in fishes.' *Science*, **136**, 157–8.

[20] BEACHER. W. J. (1952). 'The role of vision in the alighting of birds.' *Science*, **115**, 607–8.

[21] BENIUC, M. (1933). 'Bewegungssehen, Verschmelzung und Moment bei Kampffischen.' *Z. vergleich. Physiol.*, **19**, 724–46.

[22] BIERENS DE HAAN, J. A. (1925). 'Experiments on vision in monkeys.' 1. 'The colour-sense of the pig-tailed Macaque (*Nemestrinus nemestrinus* L). *J. Comp. Psychol.*, **5**, 417–53.

[23] BIERENS DE HAAN, J. A. and FRIMA, M. J. (1930). 'Versuche über den Farbensinn der Lemuren.' *Z. vergleich. Physiol.*, **12**, 603–31.

[24] BIRUKOW, G. (1950). 'Vergleichende Untersuchungen über das Helligkeits – und Farbensehen bei Amphibien. *Z. vergleich. Physiol.*, **32**, 348–82.

[25] BIRUKOW, G. and KNOLL, M. (1952). 'Tages und Dämmerungs-sehen von Froschlarven nach Aufzucht in verschiedenen Licht-bedingungen.' *Naturwiss.*, **21**, 494–5.

[26] BISHOP, P. O., KOZAK, W. and VAKKUR, G. J. (1962). 'Some quantitative aspects of the cat's eye: axis and plane of reference, visual field co-ordinates and optics.' *J. Physiol.*, **163**, 466–502.

[27] BLISS, A. F. (1946). 'Chemistry of daylight vision.' *J. Gen. Physiol.*, **29**, 277–97.

[28] BLOUGH, D. S. (1955). 'Method for tracing dark adaptation in the pigeon.' *Science*, **121**, 703–4.

[29] BLOUGH, D. S. (1957). 'Spectral sensitivity in the pigeon.' *J. Opt. Soc. America*, **47**, 827–33.

[30] *Bonaventure*, N. (1959). 'Sur la sensibilité spectrale et la

vision des couleurs chez le spermophile' (*Citellus citellus* L). *C. R. Soc. Biol.*, **153**, 1,594.

[31] BONAVENTURE, N. (1961). 'Sur la sensibilité spectrale de l'appareil visuel chez la souris. *C. R. Soc. Biol.*, **155**, 918–21.

[32] BONAVENTURE, N. (1961). 'La vision des couleurs chez le Chat.' *Rev. Psychol. Franç.*, **6**, 1–10.

[33] BONAVENTURE, N. (1962. 'Sensibilité spectrale et vision des couleurs chez le Chat.' *Rev. Psychol. Franç.*, **7**, 75–82.

[34] BORNSCHEIN, H. and SZEGVÁRI, GY. (1958). 'Flimmerelektroretinographische Studie bei einem Säuger mit reinem Zapfennetzhaut' (*Citellus citellus* L). *Z. Biol.*, **110**, 285–90.

[35] BOULET, P. (1955). 'Expériences sur la perception visuelle du mouvement sinusoïdal chez *Perca fluviatilis* L.' *C. R. Soc. Biol.*, **149**, 392–5.

[36] BRIDGES, C. D. B. (1959). 'The visual pigments of some common laboratory animals.' *Nature*, **184**, 1,727–8.

[37] BRIDGES, C. D. B. (1962). 'Visual pigment 544, a presumptive cone pigment from the retina of the pigeon.' *Nature*, **195**, 40–42.

[38] BROWN, K. T. and WATANABE, K. (1962). 'Isolation and identification of a receptor potential from the pure-cone fovea of the monkey retina.' *Nature*, **193**, 958–60.

[39] BROWN, K. T. and WATANABE, K. (1962). 'Rod receptor potential from the retina of the night monkey.' *Nature*, **196**, 547–50.

[40] BURIAN, H. M. (1939). 'The influence of the central nervous system on the pigment migration in the retina of the frog.' *Amer. J. Ophthal.*, **22**, 16–26.

[41] CAMA, H. R., DALVI, P. D., MORTON, R. A., SALAH, M. K., STEINBERG, G. R. and STUBBS, A. L. (1952). 'Studies on vitamin A. 19. Preparation and properties of retinene.' *Biochem. J.*, **52**, 535–40.

[42] CHALMERS, E. L. (1952). 'Monocular and binocular cues in the perception of size and distance.' *Amer. J. Psychol.*, **65**, 415–23.

[43] CHARPENTIER, G. (1936). 'Das Elektroretinogramm normaler und hemeraloper Ratten.' *Acta Ophthal.*, *Suppl.* **9**.

[44] CHIEVITZ, J. H. (1889). 'Untersuchungen über die Area centralis retinae.' *Arch. Anat. Physiol.*, *Anat abt.*, *Suppl.* **139**.

[45] CINAT-TOMSON, H. (1926). 'Die geschlechtliche Zuchtwahl beim Wellensittich (*Melopsittacus undulatus* Shaw).' *Biol. Zentralbl.*, **46**, 543–52.

[46] COLE. J. (1953). 'The relative importance of colour and form in discrimination learning in monkeys.' *J. Comp. Psychol.*, **15**, 16–18.

114 · REFERENCES

[47] COLEMAN, T. B. and HAMILTON, W. F. (1933). 'Color blindness in the rat.' *J. Comp. Psychol.*, **15**, 177–31.

[48] COLLINS, F. D., LOVE, R. M. and MORTON, R. A. (1953). 'Studies in vitamin A. 25. Visual pigment in tadpoles and adult frogs.' *Biochem. J.*, **53**, 632–6.

[49] COLVIN, S. S. and BURFORD, C. C. (1909). 'The color perception of three dogs, a cat and a squirrel. *Psychol. Monogr.* **11**, 1–48.

[50] CRESCITELLI, F. (1956). 'The nature of the lamprey visual pigment.' *J. gen. Physiol.*, **39**, 423–35.

[51] CRESCITELLI, F. (1958). 'The natural history of visual pigments.' *Ann. N. Y. Acad. Sci.*, **74**, 230–55.

[52] CRESCITELLI, F. and DARTNALL, H. J. A. (1953). 'Human visual purple.' *Nature*, **172**, 195–6.

[53] CROZIER, W. J. and WOLF, E. (1939). 'The flicker response contour for the gecko (rod retina).' *J. Gen Physiol.*, **22**, 555–66.

[54] CROZIER, W. J., WOLF, E. and ZERRAHN-WOLF, G. (1939). 'Flicker response function for the turtle *Pseudemys*.' *J. Gen. Physiol.*, **22**, 311–40.

[55] DARTNALL, H. J. A. (1952). 'Visual pigment 467, a photosensitive pigment present in tench retinae.' *J. Physiol.*, **116**, 257–89.

[56] DARTNALL, H. J. A. (1953). 'The interpretation of spectral sensitivity curves.' *Brit. Med. Bull.*, **9**, 24–30.

[57] DARTNALL, H. J. A. (1956). 'Further observations on the visual pigments of the clawed toad, *Xenopus laevis*.' *J. Physiol.*, **134**, 327–38.

[58] DARTNALL, H. J. A. (1960). 'Visual pigment from a pure-cone retina.' *Nature*, **188**, 475–9.

[59] DARTNALL, H. J. A. (1962). 'The identity and distribution of visual pigments in the animal kingdom.' *The Eye*, ed. Davson, Academic Press, Ch. **18**, 367–426.

[60] DARTNALL, H. J. A., LANDER, M. R. and MUNZ, F. W. (1961). 'Periodic changes in the visual pigment of a fish .'*Progress in Photobiology*, ed. Christensen and Buchmann, 203–13.

[61] DENTON, E. J. (1956). 'The responses of the pupil of *Gekko gekko* to external light stimulus.' *J. Gen. Physiol.*, **40**, 201–16.

[62] DENTON, E. J. and WARREN, F. J. (1957). 'The photosensitive pigments in the retinae of deep-sea fish.' *J. Mar. Biol. Assoc. U.K.*, **36**, 651–62.

[63] DENTON, E. J. and WYLLIE, J. H. (1955). 'Study of the photosensitive pigments in the pink and green rods of the frog.' *J. Physiol.*, **127**, 81–89.

[64] DETWILER, S. R. (1924). 'Studies on the retina: observations on the rods of nocturnal mammals.' *J. Comp. Neurol.*, **37**, 481–9.

[65] DETWILER, S. R. (1944). 'Excitation and retinal pigment migration in the frog.' *J. Comp. Neurol.*, **81**, 137–45.

[66] DETWILER, S. R. and LEWIS, R. W. (1926). 'Temperature and retinal pigment migration in the eyes of the frog.' *J. Comp. Neurol.*, **41**, 153–69.

[67] DIMELOW, E. J. (1963). 'Observations on the feeding of the hedgehog (*Erinaceus europaeus* L.).' *Proc. Zool. Soc. London*, **141**, 291–309.

[68] DODT, E. (1961). 'Elektroretinographische Untersuchungen über das adaptive Verhalten tierischer Netzhäute.' *Freiburg Symposium on Neurophysiology and Psychophysics*, 64–74.

[69] DODT, E. and ECHTE, K. (1961). 'Dark and light adaptation in pigmented and white rat as measured by electroretinogram threshold.' *J. Neurophysiol.*, **24**, 427–45.

[70] DODT, E. and ELENIUS, V. (1956). 'Spektrale Sensitivität einzelner Elemente der Kaninchennetzhaut.' *Pflüger's Arch.*, **262**, 301–6.

[71] DODT, E. and HECK, J. (1954). 'Einflüsse des Adaptationszustandes auf die Rezeption intermittierender Lichtreize.' *Pflüger's Arch.*, **259**, 212–25.

[72] DODT, E. and JESSEN, K. H. (1961). 'The duplex nature of the retina of the nocturnal gecko as reflected in the electroretinogram.' *J. Gen. Physiol.*, **44**, 1,143–58.

[73] DODT, E. and JESSEN, K. H. (1961). 'Das adaptive Verhalten der Froschnetzhaut untersucht mit der Methode der konstanten elektrischen Antwort.' *Vision Res.*, **1**, 228–43.

[74] DODT, E. and WALTHER, J. B. (1958). 'Photopic sensitivity mediated by visual purple.' *Experientia*, **14**, 142

[75] DODT, E. and WALTHER, J. B. (1958). 'Flourescence of the crystalline lens and electroretinographic sensitivity determinations.' *Nature*, **181**, 286–7.

[76] DODT, E. and WALTHER, J. B. (1959). 'Über die spektrale Empfindligheit und die Schwelle von Gecko-Augen.' *Pflüger's Arch.*, **268**, 204–12.

[77] DODT, E. and WIRTH, A. (1953). 'Differentiation between rods and cones by flicker electroretinography in pigeon and guinea-pig.' *Acta Physiol. Scand.*, **30**, 80–89.

[78] DONNER, K. O. (1953). 'The spectral sensitivity of the pigeon's retinal elements.' *J. Physiol.*, **122**, 524–37.

[79] DOWLING, J. E. and WALD, G. (1958). 'Vitamin A deficiency and night blindness.' *Proc. Nat. Acad. Sci. N.Y.*, **44**, 648–61.

[80] DUIJM, M. (1958). 'On the position of a ribbon-like central area in the eyes of some birds.' *Arch. Neerl. Zool.*, **13**, Suppl. 1. 128–45.

[81] DUKE-ELDER, S. (1958). *System of Ophthalmology* 1. *The Eye in Evolution.* Henry Kimpton, London.

[82] ELENIUS, V. and DODT, E. (1960). 'Dunkeladaptation und Duplizitätslehre.' *Pflüger's Arch.*, **272**, 20.

[83] ELENIUS, V and HECK, J (1958). 'Vergleich zwischen der *b*-Wellenamplitude und dem Verlauf der Sehpurpurregeneration bei Achromaten und Gesunden.' *Ophthalmologica*, **136**, 145–50.

[84] FORBES, A., FOX, S., MILBURN, N. and DEANE, H. W. (1960). 'Electroretinograms and spectral sensitivities of some diurnal lizards.' *J. Neurophysiol.*, **23**, 62–73.

[85] FRIDERICIA, L. S. and HOLM, E. (1925). 'Influence of deficiency of fat-soluble A vitamin in the diet on the visual purple in the eyes of rats.' *Amer. J. Physiol.*, **73**, 63–78.

[86] GOODGE, W. R. (1960). 'Adaptations for amphibious vision in the dipper (*Cinclus mexicanus*).' *J. Morphol.*, **107**, 79–91.

[87] GÖTZ, W. (1926). 'Vergleichende Untersuchungen zur Psychologie der optischen Wahrnehmungsvorgänge. 1. Experimentelle Untersuchungen zum Problem der Sehgrössenkonstanz beim Haushuhn.' *Z. Psychol.*, **99**, 247–60.

[88] GRANIT, R. (1941). 'Isolation of colour-sensitive elements in a mammalian retina.' *Acta Physiol. Scand.*, **2**, 93–109.

[89] GRANIT, R. (1941). 'Relation between rod and cone substances based on the scotopic and photopic spectra of *Cyprinus*, *Tinca*, *Anguilla* and *Testudo*.' *Acta Physiol. Scand.*, **2**, 334–46.

[90] GRANIT, R. (1942). 'Spectral properties of the visual receptor elements of the guinea-pig. *Acta Physiol. Scand.*, **3** 318–28.

[91] GRANIT, R. (1942). 'The photopic spectrum of the pigeon. *Acta Physiol. Scand.*, **4**, 118–24.

[92] GRANIT, R. (1943). 'Spectral properties of visual receptors of the cat.' *Acta Physiol. Scand.*, **5**, 219–29.

[93] GRANIT, R. (1947). *Sensory Mechanisms of the Retina.* Oxford Univ. Press, London.

[94] GRANIT, R. and SVAETICHIN, G. (1939). 'Principles and technique of the electrophysiological analysis of colour reception with the aid of micro-electrodes. *Upsala Läkaref. förh.*, **65**, 161–77.

[95] GREGG, F. M., JAMISON, E., WILKIE, R. and RADINSKY, T. (1929). 'Are dogs, cats and racoons color blind?' *J. Comp. Psychol.*, **9**, 379–95.

[96] GROSS, O. (1906). 'Untersuchungen über das Verhalten der Pupille auf Lichteinfall nach Durchschneidung des Sehnerven beim Hunde. *Pflüger's Arch.*, **112**, 302–10.

[97] GRZIMEK, B. (1952). 'Versuche über das Farbensehen von Pflanzenessern. I Das farbige Sehen von Pferde. *Z. Tierpsychol.*, **9**, 23–39.

[98] GUNTER, R. (1951). 'The absolute threshold for vision in the cat.' *J. Physiol.*, **114**, 8–15.

[99] GUNTER, R. (1954). 'The discrimination between lights of different wave-lengths in the cat.' *J. Comp, Physiol. Psychol.*, **47**, 169–72.

[100] HAMBURGER, V. (1926). 'Versuche über Komplementär-Farben bei Ellritzen (*Phoxinus laevis*).' *Z. vergleich. Physiol.*, **4**, 286–304.

[101] HAMILTON, W. F. and COLEMAN, T. B. (1933). 'Trichromatic vision in the pigeon as illustrated by the spectral discrimination curve.' *J. Comp. Psychol.*, **15**, 183–91.

[102] HARTLINE, H. K. (1940). 'Receptive fields of optic nerve fibers.' *Amer. J. Physiol.*, **130**, 690–9.

[103] HELMHOLTZ, H. VON (1867). *Handbuch der physiologischen Optik.* 1st edn. 272–309. Leipzig.

[104] HERING, E. (1920). *Grundzüge der Lehre vom Lichtsinn.* Springer, Berlin.

[105] HERMANN, G. (1958). 'Beiträge zur Physiologie des Rattenauges.' *Z. Tierpsychol.*, **15**, 462–518.

[106] HERTER. K. (1930). Weitere Dressurversuche an Fischen. *Z. wiss. Biol.*, abt. C., **11**, 730–48.

[107] HERTZ, M. (1928). 'Wahrnehmungspsychologische Untersuchungen am Eichelhähern.' *Z. wiss. Biol.* abt. C., **7**, 617–56.

[108] HESS, C. VON (1912). 'Vergleichende Physiologie des Gesichtsinnes.' *Handbuch der vergleichenden Physiologie*, ed. Winterstein, **4**, 1–290, Fischer, Jena.

[109] HESS, E. H. and GOGEL, W. C. (1954). 'Natural preferences of the chick for objects of different colors.' *J. Psychol.*, **38**, 483–93.

[110] HOLM, E. (1925). 'Demonstration of hemeralopia (night blindness) in rats nourished on food devoid of fat-soluble A vitamin.' *Amer. J. Physiol.*, **73**, 79–84.

[111] HONIGMANN, H. (1921). 'Untersuchungen über Lichtempfindlichkeit und Adaptierung des Vogelauges.' *Pflüger's Arch.*, **189**, 1–72.

[112] HORIO, G. (1938). 'Die Farb- und Formdressur an Karpfen.' *Jap.' Med. Sci.*, Part III, **4**, 395–402.

[113] HUBBARD, R. and KROPF, A. (1959). 'Molecular aspects of visual excitation.' *Ann. N. Y. Acad. Sci.*, **81**, 388–98.

[114] HUBEL, D. H. (1959). 'Single unit activity in striate cortex of unrestrained cats.' *J. Physiol.*, **147**, 226–38.

[115] HURVICH, L. M. and JAMESON, D. (1951). 'A psychophysical

I

study of white. 3. Adaptation as variant.' *J. Opt. Soc. America*, 41, 787–801.

[116] HURVICH, L. M. and JAMESON, D. (1957) 'An opponent process theory of color vision.' *J. Psychol. Rev*, 64, 384–404.

[117] INGVAR, D. H. (1959). 'Spectral sensitivity as measured in cerebral visual centres.' *Acta Physiol. Scand.*, 46, Suppl. 159.

[118] JERISON, H. J., GOLDZBAND, M. G. and CLARKE, G. (1952). 'Critical flicker fusion in the rat.' *Fed. Proc.*, 11, 78.

[119] KAESS, W. and KAESS, F. (1960). 'Perception of apparent movement in the common toad.' *Science*, 132, 953.

[120] KOLMER, W. (1924). 'Über das Auge des Eisvogels (*Alcedo attis attis*).' *Pflüger's Arch.*, 204, 266–74.

[121] KOLOSVÁRY, G. (1934). 'A study of color vision in the mouse (*Mus musculus* L) and the souslik (*Citellus citellus* L).' *J. Gen. Psychol.*, 44, 473–77.

[122] KRIES, J. VON (1896). 'Über die Funktion der Netzhautstäbchen.' *Z. Psychol.*, 9, 81.

[123] KUHN, O. and KÄHLING, J. (1954). 'Augenrückbildung und Lichtsinn bei *Anoptichthys jordani* Hubbs and Innes.' *Experientia*, 10, 385–8.

[124] LACK, D. (1943). *The Life of the Robin*. London.

[125] LASHLEY, K. S. (1916). 'The color vision of birds. I. The spectrum of the domestic fowl.' *J. Animal Behav.*, 6, 1–26.

[126] LETTVIN, J. Y., MATURANA, H. R., MCCULLOCH, W. S. and PITTS, W. H. (1959). 'What the frog's eye tells the frog's brain.' *Proc. Inst. Radio Engin.*, 47, 1940–51.

[127] LETTVIN, J. Y., MATURANA, H. R., PITTS, W. H. and MCCULLOCH, W. S. (1961). 'Two remarks on the visual system of the frog.' *Sensory Communication* ed. Rosenblith, 757–76.

[128] LEVINE, J. (1955). 'Consensual pupillary reflex in birds.' *Science*, 122, 690.

[129] LINSDALE, J. M. (1946). *The California Ground Squirrel*. Univ. Calif. Press.

[130] LOCHER, C. J. S. (1933). *Untersuchungen über den Farbensinn von Eichhörnchen*. Leiden.

[131] LOCKIE, J. D. (1952). 'A comparison of some aspects of the retinae of the Manx shearwater, fulmar petrel and house sparrow.' *Quart. J. Microscop. Sci.*, 93, 347–56.

[132] LOEVENICH, H. K. (1948). 'Die Steuerung der Zapfen- und Stäbchenbewegung in der froschnetzhaut.' *Pflüger's Arch.*, 249, 539–59.

[133] LYTHGOE, R. J. (1937). 'The absorption spectra of visual purple and of indicator yellow.' *J. Physiol.*, 89, 331–58.

[134] MACNICHOL, E. J. and SVAETICHIN. G. (1958). 'Electric responses from the isolated retinas of fishes.' *Amer. J. Ophthal.*, **46**, 26–40.

[135] MATURANA, H. R. and FRENK, S. (1963). 'Directional movement and horizontal edge detectors in the pigeon retina.' *Science*, **142**, 977–9.

[136] MATURANA, H. R., LETTVIN, J. Y., MCCULLOCH, W. S. and PITTS. W. H. (1960). 'Anatomy and physiology of vision in the frog (*Rana pipiens*)' Second Suppl. on Mechanisms of Vision. *J. Gen. Physiol.*, **43**, 129–75.

[137] MEESTERS, A. (1940). 'Über die Organisation des Gesichtfeldes der Fische.' *Z. Tierpsychol.*, **4**, 84–149.

[138] MEYER-OEHME, D. (1957). 'Dressurversuche an Eichhörnchen zur Frage ihres Helligkeits- und Farbensehen. *Z. Tierpsychol.*, **14**, 473–509.

[139] MEYKNECHT, J. (1941). 'Farbensehen und Helligkeitsunterscheidung beim Steinkauz (*Athena noctua vidalii* A. E. Brehm).' *Ardea*, **30**, 129–70.

[140] MICHELS, K. M., FISCHER, B. E. and JOHNSON, J. I. (1960). 'Raccoon performance on color discrimination problems.' *J. Comp. Physiol. Psychol.*, **53**, 379–80.

[141] MILES, P. C., RATOOSH, P. and MEYER, D. R. (1956). 'Absence of color vision in the guinea-pig.' *J. Neurophysiol.*, **19**, 254–8.

[142] MILLOT, N. and YOSHIDA, M. (1959). 'The photosensitivity of the sea urchin, *Diadema antillarum* Philippi: Responses to increases in light intensity.' *Proc. Zool. Soc. Lond.*, **133**, 67–71.

[143] MÜLLER, D. (1930). 'Sinnesphysiologische und psychologische Untersuchungen an Musteliden.' *Z. vergleich. Physiol.*, **12**, 293–328.

[144] MUNK, O. (1963). The eye of *Stomias boa ferox* Reinhardt *Vidensk. Medd. Dansk, naturh. Foren.*, **125**, 353–9.

[145] MUNTZ, W. R. A. (1962). 'Microelectrode recordings from the diencephalon of the frog (*Rana pipiens*) and a blue-sensitive system.' *J. Neurophysiol.*. **25**, 699–711.

[146] MUNTZ, W. R. A. (1962). 'Effectiveness of different colours of light in releasing positive phototactic behaviour of frogs, and a possible function of the retinal projection to the diencephalon.' *J. Neurophysiol.*, **25**, 712–20.

[147] MUNTZ, W. R. A. (1963). 'The development of phototaxis in the frog (*Rana temporaria*).' *J. Exp. Biol.*, **40**, 371–79.

[148] MUNTZ, W. R. A. (1963). 'Phototaxis and green rods in urodeles.' *Nature*, **199**, 620.

[149] MUNZ, F. W. (1958). 'The photosensitive retinal pigments of fishes from relatively turbid coastal waters.' *J. Gen. Physiol.*, **42**, 445–59.

[150] MUNZ, F. W. (1958). 'Photosensitive pigments from the retinae of certain deep-sea fishes.' *J. Physiol.*, **140**, 220–35.

[151] MUSOLFF, W. (1955). 'Untersuchungen über Farbensinn und Purkinjesches Phänomen bei drei ökologisch verschiedenen Typen der Echsen (*Lacertilia*) mit Hilfe der optomotorischen Reaktion.' *Zool. Beitr.*, **1**, 399–426.

[152] NEUWEILER, G. (1962). 'Bau und Leistung des Flughundauges (*Pteropus giganteus gig* Brünn).' *Z. vergleich. Physiol.*, **46**, 13–56.

[153] NICHOLLS, J. V. V. (1938). 'The effect of section of the posterior ciliary arteries in the rabbit.' *Brit. J. Ophthal.*, **22**, 672–87.

[154] NICKEL, E. (1960). 'Untersuchungen über den Farbensinn junger Alligatoren.' *Z. vergleich. Physiol.*, **43**, 37–47.

[155] NICOL, J. A. C. (1961). 'The tapetum in *Scyliorhinus canicula.* *J. Mar. biol. Assoc. U.K.*, **41**, 271–7.

[156] O'DAY, K. (1936). 'A preliminary note on the presence of double cones and oil droplets in the retina of marsupials.' *J. Anat.*, **70**, 465–7.

[157] O'DAY, K. (1938). 'The visual cells of the platypus (*Ornithornyncus*).' *Brit. J. Ophthal.*, **22**, 321–8.

[158] PARSONS, J. H. (1927). *An Introduction to the Theory of Perception*. Camb. Univ. Press.

[159] PENNYCUICK, C. J. (1960). 'The physical basis of astro-navigation in birds: theoretical considerations.' *J. Exp. Biol.*, **37**, 573–93.

[160] PLATH, M. (1935). 'Über das Farbunterscheidungsvermögen des Wellensittichs.' *Z. vergleich. Physiol.*, **22**, 691–708.

[161] PORTIER, A. (1923). 'La vision chez le fou de Bassan.' *Rev. Franç. d'Ornith.*, **15**, 99.

[162] PUMPHREY, R. J. (1948). 'The theory of the fovea.' *J. Exp. Biol.*, **25**, 299–312.

[163] PURKINJE, J. E. (1825). 'Beobachtungen und Versuche zur Physiologie der Sinne,' in *Neue Beiträge zur Kenntnis des Sehens*. Berlin.

[164] QUARANTA, J. V. (1949). 'The color discrimination of *Testudo vicina.*' *Anat. Rec.*, **105**, 510–11.

[165] QUARANTA, J. V. (1952). 'An experimental study of the color vision of the giant tortoise. *Zoologica*, **37**, 295–311.

[166] REEVES, C. D. (1919). 'Discrimination of light of different wave-lengths by fish.' *Behav. Monogr.*, **4**, no3,

[167] RÉVÉSZ, G. (1921). 'Tierpsychologische Untersuchungen

(Versuch an Hühnern).' *Z. Physiol. Psychol Sinnesorgane*, abt 1. **87**, 130–7.

[168] ROAF, H. E. (1933). 'Colour vision.' *Physiol. Rev.*, **13**, 43–79.

[169] ROCHON-DUVIGNEAUD, A. (1943). *Les Yeux et la Vision des Vertébrés*. Masson et Cie. Paris.

[170] RUSHTON, W. A. H. (1953). 'The measurement of rhodopsin in the living eye.' *Acta physiol. Scand.*, **29**, 16–18.

[171] RUSHTON, W. A. H. (1956). 'The difference spectrum and the photosensitivity of rhodopsin in the living human eye.' *J. Physiol.*, **134**, 11–29.

[172] RUSHTON, W. A. H. (1958). Kinetics of cone pigments measured objectively on the living human retina. *Ann. N. Y. Acad. Sci.*, **74**, 291–304.

[173] SÄLZLE, K. (1936). 'Untersuchungen über das Farbensehvermögen von Opossum, Waldmäusen, Rötelmäusen und Eichhörnchen.' *Z. Säugertierk.* **11**, 106–48.

[174] SAMOILOFF, A. and PHEOPHILAKTOVA, A. (1907). 'Über die Farbenwahrnehmung beim Hunde.' *Zentralbl. Physiol.*, **21**, 133–9.

[175] SAXÉN, L. (1956). 'The initial formation and subsequent development of the double visual cells in amphibia.' *J. Embryol. Exp. Morphol.*, **4**, 57–65.

[176] SCHULTZE, M. (1866). 'Zur Anatomie und Physiologie der Retina.' *Arch, Mikroskop. Anat.*, **2**, 165–74; 175–286.

[177] SPENCE, K. W. (1934). 'Visual acuity and its relation to brightness in chimpanzee and man.' *J. Comp. Psychol.*, **18**, 333–61.

[178] SVAETICHIN, G. and MACNICHOL, E. F. (1958). 'Retinal mechanisms for chromatic and achromatic vision.' *Ann. N.Y. Acad. Sci.*, **74**, 385–404.

[179] TANSLEY, K. (1931). 'The regeneration of visual purple with special reference to dark adaptation and night blindness.' *J. Physiol.*, **71**, 442–58.

[180] TANSLEY, K. (1956). 'Comparison of the *lamina cribrosa* in mammalian species with good and with indifferent vision.' *Brit. J. Ophthal.*, **40**, 178–82.

[181] TANSLEY, K. (1957). 'Some observations on mammalian cone electroretinograms.' *Bibl. Ophthal.*, **48**, 7–14.

[182] TANSLEY, K. (1959). 'The retina of two nocturnal geckos, *Hemidactylus turcicus* and *Tarentola mauritanica*.' *Pflüger's Arch.*, **268**, 213–20.

[183] TANSLEY, K., COPENHAVER, R. M. and GUNKEL, R. D. (1961). 'Some aspects of the electroretinographic response of the American red squirrel, *Tamiasciurus hudsonicus loquax*.' *J. Cell. Comp. Physiol.*, **57**, 11–19.

[184] TANSLEY, K., COPENHAVER, R. M. and GUNKEL, R. D. (1961). 'Spectral sensitivity curves of diurnal squirrels.' *Vision Res.*, **1**, 154–65.

[185] THOMAS, E. (1953). 'Zum "Farbensinn" einiger Bufoniden.' *Naturwiss.*, **40**, 322–3.

[186] THOMSON, L. C. (1953). 'The localization of function in the rabbit retina.' *J. Physiol.*, **119**, 191–209.

[187] THOMSON, L. C. and WRIGHT, W. D. (1953). 'The convergence of the tritanopic confusion loci and the derivation of the fundamental response functions.' *J. Opt. Soc. America*, **43**, 890–4.

[188] TIGGES, J. (1963). 'Untersuchungen über den Farbensinn von *Tupaia glis* (Diard 1820).' *Z. Morphol. Anthropol.*, **53**, 109–23.

[189] TINBERGEN, N. (1951). *The Study of Instinct.* Oxford Univ. Press.

[190] UNDERWOOD, G. (1951). 'Reptilian retinas.' *Nature*, **167**, 183–5.

[191] UNDERWOOD, G. (1954). 'On the classification and evolution of geckos.' *Proc. Zool. Soc. Lond.*, **124**, 469–92.

[192] VALENTIN, G. (1879). 'Ein beitrag zur Kenntnis der Brechungsverhältnisse der Thiergewebe.' *Pflüger's Arch.*, *19*, 78–105.

[193] VALENTIN, G. (1879). 'Fortgesetzte Untersuchungen über die Brechungsverhaltnisse der Thiergewebe.' *Pfluger's Arch.*, **20**, 283–314.

[194] VILTER, V. (1953). 'Existence d'une rètine à plusieurs mosaïques photoréceptrices chez un poisson abyssal bathéyplagique *Bathylagus benedicti*.' *C. R. Soc. Biol.*, **147**, 1,937–9.

[195] VILTER, V. (1954). 'Différenciation foveale dans l'appareil visuel d'un poisson abyssal, le *Bathylagus benedicti*.' *C. R. Soc. Biol.*, **148**, 59–63.

[196] WAGNER, H. (1932). 'Ueber den Farbensinn der Eidechsen.' *Z. vergleich. Physiol.*, **18**, 378–92.

[197] WALD, G. (1935). 'Carotenoids and the visual cycle.' *J. Gen. Physiol.*, **19**, 351–71.

[198] WALD, G. (1938). 'On rhodopsin in solution.' *J. Gen. Physiol.*, **21**, 795–832.

[199] WALD, G. (1939). 'Porphyropsin visual system.' *J. Gen. Physiol.*, **22**, 775–94.

[200] WALD, G., BROWN, P. K. and SMITH, P. H. (1953). 'Cyanopsin, a new pigment of cone vision.' *Science*, **118**, 505–8.

[201] WALD, G., BROWN, P. K. and SMITH, P. H. (1955). 'Iodopsin.' *J. Gen. Physiol.*, **38**, 623–81.

[202] WALK, R. D. and DODGE, S. H. (1962). 'Visual depth percep-

tion of a ten-month-old monocular human infant.' *Science*, **137**, 529–30.

[203] WALLS, G. L. (1934). 'The reptilian retina.' *Amer. J. Ophthal.*, **17**, 892–915.

[204] WALLS, G. L. (1934). 'The significance of the reptilian spectacle.' *Amer. J. Ophthal.*, **17**, 1,045–7.

[205] WALLS, C. L. (1937). 'Significance of the foveal depression.' *Arch. Ophthal. N.Y.*, **18**, 912–19.

[206] WALLS, G. L. (1940). 'Postscript on image expansion by the foveal clivus.' *Arch. Ophthal. N.Y.*, **23**, 831–2.

[207] WALLS, G. L. (1940). 'Ophthalmological implications for the early history of the snakes.' *Copeia*, 1–8.

[208] WALLS, G. L. (1963). *The Vertebrate Eye*. Hafner Publishing Co, New York and London.

[209] WALLS, G. L. and JUDD, H. D. (1933). 'The intra-ocular colour filters of vertebrates.' *Brit. J. Ophthal.*, **17**, 641–75; 705–25.

[210] WASHBURN, M. F. and ABBOT, E. (1913). 'Experiments on the brightness value of red for the light-adapted eye of the rabbit.' *J. Anim. Behav.*, **2**, 145–80.

[211] WATSON, J. B. and WATSON, M. I. (1913). 'A study of the responses of rodents to monochromatic light.' *J. Anim. Behav.*, **3**, 1–14.

[212] WEALE, R. A., (1953). 'Cone monochromatism.' *J. Physiol.*, **121**, 548–69.

[213] WEALE, R. A. (1953). 'Photochemical reactions in the living cat's retina.' *J. Physiol.*, **122**, 322–31.

[214] WEALE, R. A. (1955). 'Bleaching experiments on eyes of living guinea-pigs.' *J. Physiol.*, **127**, 572–86.

[215] WEALE, R. A. (1955). 'Bleaching experiments on eyes of living grey squirrels (*Sciurus carolinensis leucotis*).' *J. Physiol.*, **127**, 587–91.

[216] WEALE, R. A. (1955). 'Binocular vision and deep-sea fish.' *Nature*, **175**, 996.

[217] WEALE, R. A. (1956). 'Observations on the direct effect of light on the irides of *Rana temporaria* and *Xenopus laevis*.' *J. Physiol.*, **132**, 257–66.

[218] WEALE, R. A. (1958). 'Retinal summation and human visual thresholds.' *Nature*, **181**, 154–6.

[219] WEALE, R. A. (1961). 'Further studies of photo-chemical reactions in living human eyes.' *Vision Res.*, **1**, 354–78.

[220] WELSH, J. H. and OSBORNE, C. M. (1937). 'Diurnal changes in retina of the catfish, *Ameiurus nebulosus*.' *J. Comp. Neurol.*, **66**, 349–59.

[221] WOJTUSIAK, R. (1932). 'Über den Farbensinn der Schildkröten.' *Z. vergleich, Physiol.*, **18**, 393–436.

[222] WOLF, E. (1948). *The Anatomy of the Eye and Orbit.* 3rd edn. H. K. Lewis and Co Ltd, London.

[223] WOOLF, D. (1956). 'A comparative cytological study of the ciliary muscle.' *Anat. Rec.*, **124**, 145–63.

[224] WRIGHT, W. D. (1946). *Researches on Normal and Defective Colour Vision*, Henry Kimpton, London.

[225] WUNDER, W. (1925). 'Physiologische und vergleichend-anatomische Untersuchungen an der Knochenfischnetzhaut.' *Z. vergleich. Physiol.*, **3**, 1–61.

[226] YOUNG, J. Z. (1963). 'Light- and dark-adaptation in the eyes of some cephalopods.' *Proc. Zool. Soc. Lond.*, **140**, 255–72.

[227] YOUNG, T. (1807). 'On physical optics,' in *A Course of Lectures on Natural Philosophy and the Mechanical Arts.* I. ch. 37., 434–46.

Index